FURTHER
UNDERTAKINGS
of a

Dead Relative Collector

FURTHER

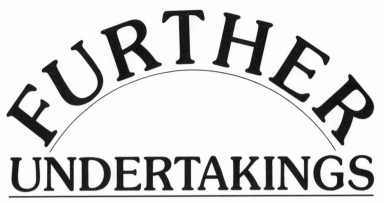

UNDERTAKINGS

of a

Dead Relative Collector

By Laverne Galeener-Moore

Illustrated by Randy Calhoun

Genealogical Publishing Co., Inc.

Published by Genealogical Publishing Co., Inc.
1001 N. Calvert Street, Baltimore, MD 21202
Second printing, 1992
Library of Congress Catalogue Card Number 88-83612
International Standard Book Number 0-8063-1246-7
Made in the United States of America

Dedicated, with All My Love, to . . .

Alan, for the ability to endure and endure and endure

Linda, for lovingly bestowing the name on me of "Grandma"

Steve, for one never knows what next

Melanie, for always bringing us so much each day . . . (from the animal hospital, and managing to get most of it off in the shower)

Julie, for hanging two more on the family tree

and

Andrew, James and *Lana, three little reasons for what it's all about*

Contents

Prolegomena   ix

Catarrh of Bile Ducts Can Lay You Low   1

Oh, Granny, Where Can Your Ashes Be? 21

Scatter! It's a Computer! 31

Will the D.O.O.D.O.O. Replace the D.A.R.? 41

Curses! An Unidentified Photograph! 55

So Your BODENSCHATZ Came from
    Rügenwaldermündenbergerfurt? 67

GAS Attacks Salt Lake City 77

Duck! It's a Minié Ball! 93

How to Make Sure Your Goal is Showing 103

Sew Those So-and-Sos Into a Quilt 117

Librarians Runnin' Wild 121

Cruising the Ohio 200 Years Later 135

Mail Monomania 149

Words to Set You Apart (Probably Far Apart) . . . 159

COLLECTING
DEAD
=RELATIVES=

FUNNY
BONE

BRIEFCASE
JAMMED
FULL WITH
FAMILY DATA

PET →

Prolegomena*

G*enealogists do so have a sense of humor!!!* Contrary to the widespread and highly discriminatory misconception held by a bunch of ignorant outsiders, we are not just a bunch of old fuddy-duddies wandering around in the advanced fog of senility, engaged in a hopelessly boring hobby. Why, some of us aren't even old. Many of the rest of us are fuddy-duddies who have managed to retain an excellent sense of humor, and kept it in pretty good working order, considering. Humor is an essential element, you see, in helping us maintain a reasonable balance between our everyday lives and our fascinating hobby, especially when other things start wearing out. Being able to laugh at ourselves may even allow us to keep a tenuous grip on our sanity and save us from the pompous fixation that genealogy is some kind of search for the Holy Grail.

---

* The use of the word "Introduction" is just too commonplace, and "Prelude" got ruled out right away because this isn't exactly a concerto you have here, just a book. The above word was finally selected after much laborious research on my part, and after some crumbs from a donut I was eating fell on the word in my thesaurus, and it looked as good a choice as any.

True, our sense of humor may be considered a tad old-fashioned. Thank goodness we do not seem to require the use of profanity with every other word or X-rated material (as hard as I hunted, I just couldn't find any in genealogy anyway) to make us break into chuckles!

Now, please forgive me, here's where I'm going to sneak in a little plug for my first book (actually my second), *Collecting Dead Relatives*. Your overwhelming response to the above book was pretty staggering. While it might sound like outright bragging, it was a real boost to the ego to find out that a dozen or so of you actually went out and bought it and found it funny (these figures are not counting my family here at home who had jolly well better laugh if they want dinner tonight). Surprisingly, the little book even did a landslide business in such exotic places as Australia, Canada and England, where the inhabitants do manage to speak a bastardized version of English. I could readily believe Australia, where they are still pretty much mavericks, even those who stop saying "G'Day" long enough to read books. And genealogists up in the frozen wasteland north of us, Canada, when they can get thawed out, probably laugh also if for no other reason than to keep their circulation going on their way to the research library through fourteen feet of snow. But I

can't understand those British. They bought the book even though some parts of it tended to be highly derogatory about the British (in one spot, as I recall, in a fit of pique, I may have even gone so far as to refer to them as Limeys, heaven forbid!), so I can't imagine what possessed them. Why, one of the British societies even got revved up to the point of writing a nice review about the book, in which they said it was "typically American in its humor" (on second thought, could that have been an insult?).

So, due to an avalanche of encouragement on the part of hordes of people (Joe at the publisher's asked, "Can you turn out another one before you dry up?", Bernie from the local store that sells typewriters and typewriter ribbons said, "With as many errors as you make, if you're doing another manuscript, that ought to be good for three or four service calls and a couple of cleaning jobs on your typewriter," and Alan, my long-suffering husband, mumbled, "I sure hope you can finish it before your family penchant for Alzheimer's Disease strikes"), I just couldn't resist being prodded into writing another book. And, with the added thrill of eager fan clubs forming in such famous places as Flatgap, Kentucky, Coon Valley, Wisconsin and Dolph, Arkansas, how could I not?

This newest book attempts to whisk you beyond the mundane, everyday chores of our glorious hobby to wildly stimulating flights of fancy in the world of digging up your dear departed at seminars, in the Mount Olympus that is Salt Lake City, and in mysterious foreign locations like Cincinnati, Ohio. To help you better understand your own physical condition (or lack thereof), and where you may be heading, there is a frightfully scientific offering about ailments, ones that laid low your ancestors and ones that may even now be latching onto you and causing you to trip along in trepidation.

For those of you who have never quite trusted the military or been able to fathom anything coming out of that particular bastion of chaos, and now sit facing your very first stuffed packet of Civil War military records concerning one of your gallant forebears, expert words of guidance are offered which, if properly studied, should be of no earthly help to you at all. If you long to become a shutterbug of the first magnitude, maybe you had better skip over the chapter on photography altogether because it just might launch you into a state of confusion.

Some of the sections make a half-hearted attempt at warning you what a nightmare you might face if you choose to preserve your genealogical collection by trotting off to a publisher. The consequences of such an action are also sprinkled here and there for you to study, and avoid.

Finally, if your present vocabulary doesn't already mark you as a person to be kept under careful observation, there is, once again, a suggested list of intellectual words in the back of the book which will be the envy of glossographers the world over, and which you can start right away in using on those individuals you have identified as being less erudite than yourself, thereby making a whale of an impression.

So, go ahead, turn off that projector light, lay down that dusty old court docket, shove aside that mountain of Xeroxed scraps of paper, and proceed with caution . . .

"Medicine being a compendium of the successive and contradictory mistakes of medical practitioners, when we summon the wisest of them to our aid, the chances are that we may be relying on a scientific truth the error of which will be recognized in a few year's time." — Marcel PROUST

Catarrh of Bile Ducts Can Lay You Low

You might well be sitting there, with a puzzled furrow on your brow, questioning why in the world of all that's sensible would an intelligent author begin what you had hoped would be a humorous book with the hardly hilarious subject of physical maladies. Not a very bright thing to do. The selection of such a depressing opening topic would generally be a sure-fire guarantee to put the reader in a dour mood, unless he or she possessed an extremely weird and free-wheeling sense of humor. But, fellow genealogists, whether we like it or not, our hobby and our aches-and-pains hobble along hand in hand.

You have only to look around you with an unjaundiced eye and your bifocals planted firmly on your nose, the next time you find yourself in a genealogical research center, to realize that most of the inmates (even though this might not include yourself, of course) are no longer spring chickens. In fact many of them would have great difficulty in even being classed as summer hens and roost-

ers. Yes, it's a sad fact that the average genealogical society membership would probably never be mistaken for the
U.S. Olympic Team or a television aerobics class in heavy
action. To be brutally frank, the old projector handle no
longer flips around with the verve it once did, the stairs to
the library are growing longer and harder to climb each
year, and the powers-that-be are definitely using smaller
print in books and fainter print on films. Accordingly,
since I just returned from a visit to my doctor, gratefully
clutching a fresh arthritis prescription which should allow
me to continue hunt-and-peck typing for another two
weeks, I decided that it seemed like a rip-roaring idea to
jump (albeit semi-agilely and while I still can) into this
genealogy book with a detailed look at not
only what can go haywire with that once
fine-tuned machine known as the genealogy
hobbyist but also at what strange afflictions
floored our predecessors.

Now that we're all thoroughly depressed,
let's take a good, honest look at ourselves.
Heaven knows, we get little reminders every
day. As an example, as soon as I had completed an intellectual perusal of the questionnaire sent some months ago to all eager
genealogists contemplating a group trip to
the Ultimate Nirvana, Salt Lake City (see
page 77), I knew
there was a crying
need for this chap-
ter. Granted, I
suppose that the
tour leader felt it
her bounden duty
to ask *some* ques-

tions (which is sort of *de rigueur* for a questionnaire, one must admit) of each person about to embark as a fellow traveler in her little coterie, and I doubt that she was suffering from a morbid curiosity, but the drift of the questions seemed a trifle unbalanced, or perhaps I should say they were heavily skewed in one direction. Whatever. There was, of course, the standard space for one's name (no "anonymous" monkey business here, you can bet, and this was undoubtedly so they could stick a name-tag on you so you wouldn't forget); your home address (in case you couldn't recollect it upon your return after a solid week of projector crank-turning fatigue); your home telephone number (to discourage you from making long distance calls home from your hotel room and then skipping out without paying). Altogether these brief inquiries took up very little space at all on the questionnaire, but the remainder of the sheet resembled a witch-hunt into your innermost secrets, as represented by the following questions:

1. List all your health problems, past and current (with lines and lines and lines of blanks to accommodate even the most meticulous hypochondriac).

2. List all medications you are presently taking or will be planning to take on this trip (again with generous blank spaces and the sincere hope that you will be able to spell the answers correctly). (I don't know, could this have been a hidden ploy by the government to perform some dastardly act of drug testing on genealogists?)

3. Please check with your doctor before you leave for his determination as to whether any of the above might cause you to have a drastic reaction at high altitude (now, I didn't think the elevation of Salt Lake City was so unusual as to require the wearing of oxygen masks, so I

guessed this question referred to those traveling by air, and I'll have to admit, no matter what they say in their ads, United Airlines personnel get decidedly *un*-friendly if a genealogist, or anyone else for that matter, runs amok in a 737, no matter what the medical reason). As it turned out, the majority of folks chose to play it safe and subsequently took the train, so perhaps there had been a legitimate concern over coming unglued.

4. Please list your next-of-kin, address, home phone number, office number, relationship to you, his or her hobbies (just in case they included manufacturing bombs, I guess). (As you can probably figure out, some questionees got all confused about this question and sent in their family chart, thinking the question genealogical, but the tour leader patiently explained that she needed a *live* next-of-kin, for reasons upon which I did not care to dwell.)

But now, a word in the defense of genealogy hobbyists . . . For all the preliminary emphasis on frailty, medical problems and possible catastrophes, I truly believe there should be a federally-funded study made on those hardy souls who frequent 35 North West Temple Street. It certainly amazed me about the patrons of the LDS Family History Library, that such a great number of them (usually of an advanced age at that) chose to arrive at 7:00 A.M. (and sometimes earlier) in order to get a good place in line (rain, snow or shine), stand feebly on one foot and then the other, undaunted (some of them were even in wheelchairs), for a half-hour or more, stampede inside when the doors opened at 7:30, and stick it out until they were forced to stagger out at 10:00 P.M. closing time. That fact has got to indicate *something* about the health, physical and mental, of most of us genealogists, don't you think?

By the way, I did hear a sigh of relief wheeze out of our tour director, who was one of the youngest and nimblest of our group, when the last of our merry little band doddered off into the sunset at the end of our exciting excursion, with no need arising for the tour director to get up-close-and-personal with anyone's next-of-kin.

Meandering along on this joyous subject of health problems, have you ever gone to a doctor's office for an initial visit, only to have a sadistic nurse thrust a six-page form into your hands and brusquely order you to fill in each blank completely? Well, you may not even be certain you can correctly supply the answers to the easy questions, such as, "Did you have head lice between the ages of five and fourteen?" or "When you were an infant, did you suffer from excrementitious problems, either blockages or diarrheic, and if so, why?" Even if you can somehow figure out answers to these little gems, what do you do about the real stumpers, such as, "Which of the following diseases did your grandmother have?", followed by twenty-five choices. Why, some of us never even met our grandparents, much less hung around long enough to listen to them discourse much about their innards. But here is where we genealogy freaks are one horse ahead of the rest of the merry-go-round, simply because of the snoopy nature of our hobby itself. The person committed to genealogy is a privileged individual indeed. By his or her own prying, he or she can become privy to such earth-shattering recorded revelations as to what (or who) killed one's ancestors, and other people's ancestors as well, which information can then be used as a titillating topic of conversation at dinner parties.

Therefore, in the course of your genealogical research, if you have reached a stalemate with a certain branch, as we all tend to do if we live long enough, you can always pull out your prize collection of death certificates and start assembling a cheery, twelve-generation chart listing what everybody died of, including contributory causes, if you really want to be thorough. That way, if insanity runs in your family, like it does in mine, you'll be prepared. If you can overcome the deep depression that is almost certain to overtake you from doing this type of research, you can look forward to the exalted honor of becoming The Recognized Authority and Top Expert in your family on death, sickness and miscellaneous mayhem involving your relatives. Living family members will automatically send you newspaper obituaries, funeral notices and snapshots of gravestones to help brighten your days. All this spirited activity should force the younger generation to look at you with a great deal of wonder, ask questions about your fascinating work, or maybe even stay out of your way altogether.

However, you'd best be prepared for certain vexatious problems once you've embarked on this type of medical research. For starters, you are probably already aware that the handwriting of modern doctors is usually so atrocious as to make future research of this kind next to impossible. But in the olden days doctors wrote carefully because they were under the silly delusion that somebody might need to read what they had written. They may not have always been too careful with spelling, which wasn't considered terribly important in pioneer times anyway, since the majority of their patients couldn't read or write, much less spell, but their writing on death certificates can usually be deciphered. On those formal documents the local doctor was undoubtedly showing off his cursive ability in front of the county clerk who usually did possess reading skills. What can't always be figured out is what in the world the good doctor meant. For instance, the physician for one unfortunate lady in our family declared he was of the opinion that her cause of death was "nervous cramp." (???) Another relative expired due to "marssonus." (???) I'm not making this stuff up. Every cause of death included in this chapter comes right smack off a death certificate I have here in my stuffed-to-the-bursting-point file cabinet.

Therefore, unless you graduated cum laude from Harvard Medical School, you have every right to ask, "How in the Sam Hill do I figure out what this means?" The medical knowledge imbued in most of us barely allows us to be able to keep up with the latest brand names of aspirin and, if we're really advanced, to figure out how to read our own personal prescription directions without assistance from a pharmacist. Unfortunately, most folks are totally in the dark when it comes to scientific terms such as nyctalopia. So it follows that the average genealogist will probably need help, or the services of a translator, before he or she can successfully chart his or her family's medical records. While it might sound like bragging, I consider myself lucky in that regard because medical expertise runs rampant in my family. Not only was my paternal grandmother a self-appointed midwife, but one of our daughters is a registered animal health technician. As a result, I've inherited the rare ability to be able to tell if the persons in old family portraits look pregnant, the ladies especially; and if any of our kinfolk were struck down with rabies or distemper, why I could probably identify those like a shot. I'm further blessed, of course, by having taken Biology 1 in high school, but try as I might, about all I can recollect from that scholarly endeavor is how to cut up a frog, which hasn't been of much use lately. But I'm sure I would be right up there with the best of them if it came to recognizing warts.

All on my own, I've figured out a brilliant solution about how to get definitions for early medical terminology. What you do is write down all the funny words you don't understand from the death certificates, save them up and, on your next trip to your own doctor, just spring them on him. That way you might get your money's worth. I realize that this kind of maneuver could be pretty tricky to accomplish, however, since most doctors strive to limit themselves to one-and-a-half minutes maximum in the examining room, so you'll have to talk fast. You could always claim that *you* have the words as symptoms. *That* might grab his attention and persuade him to stay overtime.

Among the causes throwing me for a loss was the one I included in the title of this chapter, "catarrh of bile ducts." Such a ghastly diagnosis sounds like something one wouldn't talk about in polite society, or with men around. Another family member Went to His Reward, as they were fond of saying, from "infl. of head." (???) One unfortunate gentleman in rural Missouri passed over from "percussion of the brain," and while even I could guess full well what that must have meant, the contributory cause better explained it—"injury received in blasting well." So, not only had the dynamite given those hardy pioneers a new water supply, it had dispatched Cousin Ebenezer to Kingdom Come.

One of the more common old-fashioned terms you'll stumble across was flung around far too often by early-day medics. At least it was a disease that practically everybody could learn to pronounce—"Ague." My daughter read an article recently in a medical journal (a people medical journal, not an animal one) which claimed that there was far too much frivolous use of this particular medical diagnosis. I do believe, in some cases, it may have been resorted to as a handy escape mechanism. Permit me to enlighten you.

It might come as a surprise to you, but not all frontier physicians and surgeons were Phi Beta Kappa graduates of a recognized medical school. Some of them, in fact, could barely read and write. When one of this breed was summoned to give an opinion on a fellow pioneer afflicted with rigor mortis, it could easily turn into a test of his (the doctor's) respect and standing in the community, and maybe even whether the locals would let him live to go on practicing. If he couldn't find a convenient bullet hole, protruding arrow, or some other obvious clue on the corpse, and it still possessed all its parts, more or less, he could be in big trouble, especially if he was playing the scene in front of a crowd of spectators, sometimes angry,

impatient, monster-sized *kinfolk* spectators. So, for his own safety, he would scrunch his face into a serious doctorly frown, mutter "Hmmmm, hmmmm" a couple of times while scratching his head, then adjust his spectacles on his nose and proclaim, "Ague!" Once the hangers-on had finished asking, "Whudee say?" and the doctor had quickly departed the premises, clutching his black bag and his 25¢ fee, all there remained to do was to bury the dear departed and pray nobody else got struck down with it, whatever it was. Nobody pursued it much. So, if you find this cause on an ancestor's death record, you can probably just select a disease at random.

We were certainly lucky in my family, especially back in eastern Kentucky, to have such short, precise, easy-to-understand diagnoses recorded for the expiration of numerous loved ones. "Shot died" was one of them, but most doctors probably would have felt the "died" part was a bit redundant on a death certificate, so they generally just jotted down "shot" and let it go at that. However, the local official who was in charge of the 1880 Mortality Schedule back there went out of his way (unnecessarily, I thought) to add a lot of derogatory remarks about my kinfolk, their way of life, and the passing thereof. Somehow I have a strong feeling that he could have been one of the perpetrators, as they call them on television cop shows, and was undoubtedly trying to justify why he had hidden behind the biggest tree in town and decided to be a "contributory cause" of death.

Speaking of the Mortality Schedules, some researchers deliberately ignore or simply miss these juicy little morsels altogether. Perhaps it's because people in the 1800s had to be fortunate in picking the beginning of a decade in which to croak (those whose number came up in years not ending with a zero passed in virtual obscurity). To be able to achieve the greatest publicity then, one had to resort to careful planning in order to get one's name and the attendant recognition into these prestigious government-sponsored gossip sheets. The reason they didn't hit the streets more often, I'll hazard a guess, is that it most likely took the mental giants employed in this type of federal endeavor at least ten years just to alphabetize the bloody results and figure out what to do with them. So in between times they left the members of the public strictly alone to die unheralded and in peace. Just like with the census, you could change wives, multiply, move around, or get up to all sorts of shenanigans in the offyears and the government just looked the other way. But just think what a disaster it must have been for those early enumerators when a plague or a particularly violent feud hit their county in a year ending with a zero.

If you are a diligent researcher and can somehow decipher the handwriting on the Mortality Schedules, you will be rewarded with all sorts of causes of death. As a typical example, the causes listed in order on the particular Kentucky schedule mentioned above (which included every recorded death in that lively county in 1880, not just those of my family members) were: "consumption, cerebro spinal fever, hooping cough, shot died" (this wasn't the one for my relative, but my kin probably had something to do with it because it was for a surname they frequently had in their gun-sights), "hooping cough, hooping cough, rhumatizm, apploplexe, shot, deptherie, gun shot wound, shot, shot, hooping cough, hooping cough." At a quick glance, it appears that the cautious Kentuckian in that county in that year had to be on the lookout for two main threats—respiratory germs and irritated fellows packing rods.

But you should be careful to avoid the assumption that everything you read on these official Mortality Schedules is gospel. I became suspicious of the entry for the gentleman who was listed as passing on from a gun shot wound. He was my great-grandfather's nephew and it was a fact that all the newspaper articles written at the time about him confirmed that he had gone to his eternal rest as a result of the stated gun shot wound. But I tried to keep an open mind since I was also well aware of one of my family's highly publicized hobbies, that of staging phony funerals, using rocks, I suppose, or Lord knows who as the body in the coffin. And sure enough, in this case I found the "deceased" listed over a year later, and then again two years after that, quite alive and living with his "widow" and children in a friendlier neighboring county, a known family location. Now, either this chap managed to emulate our Saviour and rise from the dead, or the rest of the family finally perfected their peculiar pastime into a rousing success.

For a really in-depth look at the unbelievable medical world your ancestors had to face, I suggest you consider the purchase of an old medical book, if you can locate one, or ask your local librarian if one is available in the rare books section. I have one here at home—*The People's Medical Adviser*—handed down (for some reason) in my husband's family, first published in 1875, with an updated second edition rolling off the press in 1895. It's a wonder any of our ancestors lived to have descendants, quite frankly, unless they kept a healthy distance from the oddballs writing such medical books. Dr. PIERCE, the illustrious author of the above tome, points an accusing finger directly at what he determined were the two main causes of most of the health problems of his day, liquor and masturbation (in no particular order). He claimed young men must simply cease and desist conjuring up pictures of naked ladies, must quit immediately the vile habit of reading "amorous stories and obscene books" (which activity he referred to as "sensual lust"), or they would be heading pell-mell down the road to ruin by way of self-abuse, which caused epilepsy, paralysis and insanity, just for starters. Further pontificating, he advised those same hot-blooded young men to pent up their "pernicious youthful habits," stop horseback riding for awhile (which was guaranteed to turn the young man into a fiend pretty fast), avoid eating late-night meals and take a cold bath every morning, all of which would give them a fighting chance of escaping a life of sin and depravity.

There is a whole section in the book, in between hundreds of grateful testimonials by those of the good doctor's patients who lived (by some miracle) and who could write, about the horrors of Alcoholic Liquors. Dr. PIERCE claimed at least one blessing was that animals had not taken to booze, "for if the evils of alcohol were

made to extend equally to animals lower than man, we should soon have none that were tameable, none that were workable, and none that were eatable." (I'm tempted to read that last passage out loud to my dog, but she's too sedated from beer to pay much attention.) The lunatic fringe running around today, screaming about animal rights, could well take a little time out from blowing up meat-packing plants and erect a statue to old Dr. PIERCE, a pioneer in the cause of animal activism if there ever was one.

The doctor hysterically went on to say that even one drachm of alcohol "immediately endangers the life of the individual." (Thank God we've stopped serving hooch in drachms, is all I can say!) He warns the reader to be constantly vigilant for he fears that poisonous alcoholic beverages can be cunningly disguised, when you're least expecting it, by tossing in treacle (yuk!), coriander or caraway seeds to trick the unsuspecting (why would you ruin good liquor by doing that?), cayenne pepper or green vitriol (that should be enough to make you take the pledge right there), so that one must never let down one's guard because even innocent-appearing tea and coffee might stimulate a person into a frenzy. Whewww! He must have gotten awfully thirsty!

There is a chapter near the back of the book about health problems peculiar to women. Most women, Dr. PIERCE informs us, have an abundance of chores to keep them busy, so have neither the time nor the mental ability to recognize an approaching health problem until it has laid them out. About all that can be done for them is to see that they keep their skin clean and, if you can catch them between chores, try to get a good tonic down them now and then. That was about all he had to offer relative to women and their strange afflictions, but it was followed

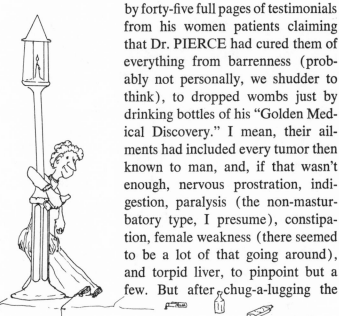

by forty-five full pages of testimonials from his women patients claiming that Dr. PIERCE had cured them of everything from barrenness (probably not personally, we shudder to think), to dropped wombs just by drinking bottles of his "Golden Medical Discovery." I mean, their ailments had included every tumor then known to man, and, if that wasn't enough, nervous prostration, indigestion, paralysis (the non-masturbatory type, I presume), constipation, female weakness (there seemed to be a lot of that going around), and torpid liver, to pinpoint but a few. But after chug-a-lugging the doctor's magic elixer, they were able to get right back to their chores without a whimper. One Sioux City, Iowa female downed nineteen bottles of the stuff at one sitting to try to cure a bladder problem and no longer could tell she had a problem at that point. There is even one testimonial in this section from a man who, presumably, wasn't suffering from female weaknesses. He claimed he just felt moved to spontaneously contribute the fact that he believed Dr. PIERCE's prescription "is the best female regulator on earth." Now, I certainly can't imagine what prompted this chap, who hailed from Mississippi and was a preacher to boot, to place himself in the limelight this way by offering up such a scandalous confession. God knows how often he felt compelled to "regulate" the women of his parish!

The doctor was no slouch when it came to diagnosing general ailments either. He said proudly that it was all due to his ability to interpret symptoms. For instance, when he noticed a patient lying on his back continuously during an acute disease, he could deduce by that symptom that the patient had "general prostration" (those who probably weren't already dead, that is). He did warn his readers that this condition could mean "the patient is sinking" (which was a safe guess). He continued, saying that most of his patients preferred to sit up (I wonder why?), so when one of them assumed a supine position, which was apparently rare, it could mean trouble. He added that you couldn't trust patients who sit up all the time either, because if they have an anxious expression on their countenance and cough fit to be tied, they could have "water about the lungs," which was just about as bad as an alcoholic beverage.

Dr. PIERCE confided in his readership that he always counted on another little scientific trick of his to help him get to the root of the problem, and that was to look at the patient's countenance to help him, the doctor, determine what was bothering the poor bloke. As an example, if there was too much contraction and expansion of the nostrils, the patient might be having trouble breathing (nowadays it would indicate he had just completed an obscene telephone call). And, if the patient had a downcast expression on his puss, wouldn't look the doctor in the eye and had a peculiar lifting of the upper lip (you guessed it), it meant one thing only—SEXUAL ABUSE (I told you this guy was really hung up on this subject). He went on to say that the patient so afflicted seemed to have a "desire to escape from conversation and to elude society" (I'll bet not *female* society). While the doctor firmly believed this particular type of patient had lost nearly all interest in the ordinary affairs of life, the poor soul was probably just looking to escape a long, boring sermon from Dr. PIERCE.

The *People's Medical Adviser* is full to bursting with drawings of revolutionary new (as of 1875 or 1895) medical machines, many of which seemed to be for the purpose of sticking up one's nose. Maybe the doctor prided himself on being a nose specialist, perhaps because of his never-ending struggle to get young men's minds off other parts of the anatomy. He devotes a mountain of space to such stimulating topics as nasal catarrh, nasal polypus, nasal tumors, nasal flushing (he actually tries to promote this deviant activity), and the nasal septum and possible deformities. Driven by this nose fetish of his, he had invented a powder which was to be used as a catarrh remedy. The sufferer was instructed to mix a whole package of the stuff with rain water or melted snow, let it settle for eight hours and stick it up his nasal passages. He further warned folks not to expect a speedy cure because

such things took time (and a lot more packages of his amazing powder, I'll bet) before the miracle cure restored one's nose to its full glory.

Any of us who have dealt with old records recognize consumption as a fairly common cause of the demise of early-day citizens. Dr. PIERCE describes the disease and generously shares with us his theories as to its causes: masturbation (you're not surprised, are you?), excessive venery (are you listening, you young dissipated men out there?), depressed mental emotions, insufficient clothing, tight lacing, and fast life in fashionable society, among other ghastly sins. So, if you find that one of your ancestors died of this cause, it should raise your eyebrows indeed, for you may have uncovered an unspeakable depravity in your family tree. I don't feel so bad now for Camille because, while the dictionary says she was a virgin of unblemished character, and while it is sad watching her waste away in that old movie, just think what a wild time she must have had previously.

You will run across the term "Dyspepsia" on old death certificates from time to time and my dictionary defines it as impaired digestion. Guess what Dr. PIERCE says causes it? Right. Masturbation, the use of alcoholic stimulants, irritability of temper, and eating fruit that isn't ripe (what kind of a moron would do that, pray tell?). I'm guessing that not too many of Dr. PIERCE's dyspepsia patients recovered because he prescribed a hydrochloric acid cocktail after each meal as a cure.

There is even a chapter in this antiquated medical book on hernias and ruptures, with drawings of unclothed men!!! No, I won't loan the book to you curious females. Besides, all the men are wearing leaves and other foliage over the interesting parts, so as not to have any readers of the weaker sex faint dead away from tremors and palpitations. After all, with all the good doctor's known hangups, he wasn't about to allow outright pornography in his book, now was he?

In between worrying about your ancestors' health problems and trying to ignore your own, gentle reader, you never know when you're going to get hit with one that suddenly demands your undivided attention. It could even interrupt the pursuit of your hobby for a time. Like just now, when I thought I'd about wrapped up this chapter, doggoned if I didn't get a bombshell in the form of a telephone call from the nurse at my doctor's office. She cheerfully informed me that they have scheduled major surgery for me ten days from now. I suspect it's a plot by the medical profession to try to stop me from writing about them. You can never tell when the AMA will strike! But my orthopedist swears I've ripped something called a rotator-cuff. (No, it's not down there, it's in my shoulder.) I guess I may have given the old projector-crank one violent turn too many. The doctor went on to give me further unpleasant details like the fact that he would be sadistically taping down my right arm (the guilty one) to my body so that I couldn't move it for six weeks! Why, that's the part of me that contains one of the two fingers I use to type! Wait till my publisher hears about that cheery development. Therefore, if this book comes to a sudden, screeching halt, you'll know why.

So as not to stop all of what is laughingly referred to as "smooth flowing continuity," it looks like I will have to depend solely on my other typing finger, and a far less humorous disposition besides, to finish the job. If the rotator-cuff in my left shoulder pulls some kind of sympathy strike, as a result of the added burden, the only choice left to me will be to dictate the rest of the book either to my dog or my husband, neither one of whom is any great shakes as a typist. This is just a small sample, fellow genealogists, of the trials and aggravations we are forced to face now and then in the pursuit of our happy hobby.

Well, now that we've bellyached about our bellyaches and tried to come to grips with early medical terminology (so as to better understand why those who departed did so), where do we head next? How about straight to the cemetery?

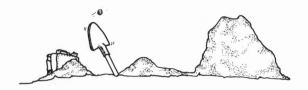

"Eternity is a terrible thought. I mean, where's it going to end?" — Tom STOPPARD

Oh, Granny, Where Can Your Ashes Be?

If you are a raw novice who has only recently infiltrated the hobby of genealogy, you may be operating under the delusion that locating an ancestor's grave is a snap. After all, you say, he surely died right there in the same county where he lived most of his life, must have been buried in the cemetery nearest to his home and, of course, there certainly had to have been an indestructable tombstone with all the proper information deeply carved on it planted at the head of the grave, right? Oh yeah! Now, here's how it sometimes was in the real world. Your ancestor could have been off in the neighboring county slaughtering Indians, when some of them reciprocated, cooked him and fed his body to the camp dogs. Or he may have run off and deserted his spouse and then who knows where he may have been when he Met His Maker? Or one or the other of the older generation may have gone a bit strange in the head toward the end of his, or her, life and been shipped off to a willing relative in another county or state, never to return, dead or alive. Or the family may have been so dirt-poor that they couldn't afford anything but a simple wooden marker, which would have long since disintegrated, or been used by some shivering traveler to start a fire. In some cases, even if those left behind had managed to scrape together enough for a stylish, permanent gravestone, later unthinking townspeople may have used the same tombstone, and a number of others like it, to lay out a sidewalk, dam a creek, or help brace up a sagging pig-pen. How's that for sacrilege? And if you're searching for someone slightly more modern, and progressive enough to be cremated, good luck, because you may need it.

At one of the genealogical societies where I had been roped into being a guest speaker, the agenda, firmly dictated by hide-bound tradition, called not only for a full recitation of the previous meeting's less-than-fascinating recorded minutes, but also a spellbinding segment devoted to allowing any fully paid-up member to perform show-and-tell right up there in front of the captive audience. One man immediately jumped up and started talking even before he'd been officially recognized, as male genealo-

gists sometimes feel the need to do if they are ever going
to get a word in edgewise. Well, it was rather obvious that
he was a beginner, wouldn't you know, as he rambled on,
filling us all in about some kind of pathetic maiden sortie
into a big library, where he probably shouldn't have been
in the first place, in downtown Los Angeles, or San Diego,
or somewhere down there in all that smog. A half-hour
later, when the gentleman finally ran out, a lady popped
up cheerfully and seemed to be accepted on the spot as a
familiar face by those of the membership who hadn't
dozed off peacefully in the comfort of the over-heated
room. I gathered, eventually, that she was an elected officer of the group. And her story appeared to have been
continued from a previous meeting because she said, "I
just wanted to keep you posted about Grandmother's
ashes. I still haven't found them. Do any of you have any
other ideas where she might be?" (???) I mean, nobody
blinked an eye and she was dead serious. For a number of
meetings, up to and including that particular one, she had
been trying to conduct what resembled a scavenger hunt
for her grandmother's ashes by soliciting the membership
for clues as to where to look next. Various members complied by offering spontaneous counseling while she took
notes. Perhaps, one said, an older relative was concealing
Granny, or what was left of her, for some unknown reason. Another cooperative soul put forth the possibility
that one of the more frugal next-of-kin may have suc-
ceeded in having the elusive ashes deposited in the grave
of another family member (a previously buried one, that
is). One of the men, going way out on a limb, advised the
woman to try to ferret out whether any of her male relatives may have had a pilot's license and some kind of
access to an airplane; if so, he may have decided to scatter
Grandmother most anywhere. Not surprisingly, there

were nearly endless theories as to what could have befallen dear old Granny. The lady with the problem ashes, her briefcase stuffed with hot new leads, promised faithfully to update everyone at the next meeting.

Speaking of mysteries involving ashes . . . Some years ago my husband and I found ourselves solely in charge of the care of an elderly uncle who had no children or other close family. The doctors kept removing things until there wasn't much left and Uncle had to go to a nursing home. In this part of California, once a house becomes vacant, it doesn't take the two-footed vermin very long to break into the said house and cart off every single item worth stealing, so we knew we had to beat them to it by ourselves carting off every single item to a storage locker. Of course, being full-fledged genealogicoholics, we kept a wary eye out for anything even vaguely smacking of family history. Well, you can imagine our shock, to say the very least, when going through a lovely antique chiffonnier, we pulled open one of the drawers and discovered what looked like a peculiar type of vase. It wasn't a vase at all, of course, but a funeral urn, a *full* funeral urn. The official explanation we found on a card accompanying the urn said the ashes were those of an infant, and the baby's mother was identified as Uncle's next-door neighbor who, we knew, was no longer alive. It had been common knowledge, we later learned, that during the time which preceded, by well over two years, this baby's birthdate, as recorded on the urn, the neighbor lady's husband had been away at sea for an extended period of time. Whose baby was it? Why did its final resting place come to be Uncle's dresser drawer? Possibly this type of discovery might not be your everyday, run-of-the-mill occurrence while doing family searching, but if you stay in this hobby long enough and you snoop around diligently enough, you'd best be prepared for little surprises of your own.

By the way, if your collecting of dead relatives actually turns up a departed family member (or someone connected to one in some way), literally, cremated or otherwise, you are going to run into some government regulations you never imagined. You can't just plant them in amongst the geraniums in your backyard, even if you do stage an appropriate religious ceremony. There are rules, it seems, for that sort of activity, and the authorities don't look too favorably on do-it-yourself projects of that nature in most communities. In the case of the baby's ashes, mentioned above, our local undertaker was able to inter them with Uncle, when his time came, and we prayed that was the right choice. After all, Uncle had chosen to be guardian of the ashes for such a long time, we felt that he might want to go on in that role. Who knows, there must have been a reason?

I can certainly sympathize and readily identify with all you genealogists who have traveled back and forth across the country in order to spend half your vacation time wandering around in cemeteries, hunting for names you recognize. On occasion that sort of pastime can really get your goat. Some years ago, when we were agile enough to get clear back to St. Clair County, Missouri, a family hangout, we went armed with all the death certificates we had rounded up for years, and even went so far as to buy a local map which included all the graveyards, old and new. Our advance planning even included a visit with a very old man who didn't have many teeth left and was the local authority on the good old days and where everybody was buried. He swore that my UNDERWOOD great-grandparents were interred right alongside one of the YOUNGER brothers who was killed in a gunfight (that would have been appropriate, I thought, considering). And, as far as my GALEENER great-grandfather was concerned, the map showed a convenient cemetery on each side of where his farm had been, so I figured it would be duck soup finding where they had put him in 1874. Accordingly, we got our cameras primed to take snapshots of gravestones and set out optimistically toward our goals.

Three days later we were covered with more chigger bites than you could count and hadn't run across a single family tombstone in any of the cemeteries we had waded through. Well, now, I take that back. Because we had brought along plenty of film, and seemed to have no legitimate use for it, we simply took pictures of nice tombstones that took our fancy, those with readable names on them, names that were at least similar to the ones we were looking for because, we figured, you can never tell. So, if the stone said HOUK, UNDERWOOD or any other vaguely familiar surname, we clicked the old camera, even if it didn't seem to make much sense. You may look down your nose at this sort of activity as being a waste of time and film, but, as it later turned out, every single one of those departed souls wound up having a tie-in with our family. Now I'm only sorry we weren't that non-selective in other graveyards we visited in so many faraway locations we'll probably never get up the gumption to go to again.

Many of you may have experienced the frustration I felt in the two cemeteries on either side of my GALEENER great-grandfather's farm. I just *knew* he had to be planted in one of them. But neither little country graveyard had very many tombstones left in it, and those that remained would never be identified with past prosperity and were slowly crumbling to pieces. Being a Californian, automatically and recognizably into weird practices, I thought if I stood very still in each cemetery and tried transcendental meditation, I'd surely receive a mystical sign of Great-Grandfather's exact location, maybe like a bolt of lightning, or an angel pointing a finger, or a ghostly voice calling out, "Hey, over here!" But the spirit world was out to lunch that day, I guess, and all was still.

The reverse emotion was felt in Fort Jefferson, Ohio in an even smaller burying spot. Two of the sturdiest tombstones in the whole place, dating back to the 1860s and in such fine shape that they will probably still be doing their duty 100 years from now, were guarding the resting places of my PARENT great-grandparents. No one can describe the euphoria that slithers up on a person who comes face-to-face with buried ancestors! I ordered my husband, who is the only one of the two of us who knows how to operate our camera professionally, to take pictures

from every angle imaginable, horizontal, vertical, semi-cockeyed, looking down from up a tree, and with me in the picture, standing stiffly between the two stones with a triumphant smirk on my face. After all, it wasn't a sight one encountered every day (unless one spent all one's time in cemeteries). It was solid, marbleized proof that I really did have great-grandparents and, by golly, they really had died and been buried! What a thrill!

In a rural county of Illinois my husband was counting on being able to purchase a map showing possible cemetery locations for *his* family members, who kept moving back and forth across the Wabash and dying on heaven knows which side of it. But no such map was available. I got what I thought was a brilliant idea and suggested we stop at the local undertaking establishment. Alan was horrified, refused to go inside with me, and slunk down low in the car seat, praying no locals would see him making a spectacle of himself. Indoors in the dim light I was met by a man in a dark suit, wearing a painfully sad expression, until it dawned on him that I wasn't there to "make arrangements," and then he broke into what had to be for him a rare grin. Granted, he probably didn't receive many social calls, but he hadn't totally forgotten how to deal with upright, non-grieving human beings. He was polite enough to offer me some kind of liquid refreshment (looking back on it, in that part of Illinois it had to have been coffee, which I don't imbibe), which was certainly acceptable behavior, and he asked me to be seated while he turned up the lights a bit so that he could draw directions to some of the old graveyards. My husband, more than a little apprehensive at the thought that I was, as usual, committing a social gaffe of the very worst kind, was relieved when I appeared on the front step of the funeral home and waved a friendly goodbye to the undertaker. He was even more relieved when I got back in the car with a hand-drawn map of the cemeteries. I include this boring little vignette, fellow genealogists, to show you that there is more than one way to skin a cat, so to speak. So, in your wanderings about the country, don't neglect morticians. They can have other uses than the one that usually leaps to mind.

You never know what road blocks will deter you from your genealogical goals. In the case of finally zeroing in on the cemetery in Illinois containing my husband's family members, even with the fresh diagram from the funeral parlor clutched in our eager hands, we ran into a road block. I mean a *real* road block. It said, "ROAD CLOSED." Now, we hadn't driven all the way back there to that Godforsaken place to be met with that kind of sign, so we just drove right around it, because that was the only road to the cemetery. It was farm country so we figured there had to be some level land upon which to drive. We did pass by the road crew, eating lunch and looking somewhat startled upon seeing our car tootling by, but we never did see any other human beings (or cops either, thank goodness). And we did find the cemetery, a tiny one nestled between a farmhouse and a running brook, and probably not too different in appearance than when the folks were buried there. We picked some wildflowers from the brookside and put them on the graves of Alan's great-grandparents and other kin, and we like to think they may have been looking down not too disapprovingly at our inherited yankee ingenuity.

Now that we've dealt for two whole chapters on diseases, death, and dying, maybe it would be nice to pick a more impersonal subject to worry about next. But, come to think about it, discussing computers ranks right up there with talking about Iran, the stock market, and higher mathematics, in my opinion anyway, and will probably put me to sleep right here at the old typewriter, which might be a blessing any way you look at it.

Scatter!
It's a Computer!

No decent genealogy book, magazine, newsletter, seminar, or conference would be worth its salt these days without offering its portion of expertise on that bugaboo of the modern world, the computer. So here goes. But first, please understand that I hate, loathe and despise computers. *And they know it!* Computers can sense an antagonist at the drop of a floppy disk. To make matters worse, computers are the supreme masters of deviousness and revenge, and they seem to have the ability to brew up all sorts of trouble. They are just lying in wait out there, ready to screw up my day. Permit me to share a shining example.

One weekday morning last summer I strolled into my friendly neighborhood grocery store, little dreaming what a massive Excedrin headache lay in wait for me. Now some of you may decide to skip this part altogether because you look upon grocery shopping as downright boring, and you may also be of the opinion that nothing that could ever happen in a grocery store, unless someone witnessed little green men pushing around a grocery cart in one, would warrant even five seconds of your time and attention. I certainly have to agree with you that the mundane practice of grocery shopping is usually a ho-hummer of the first magnitude, one which turns the participant who gets stuck with the duty into a sleep walker. So it was for me on that particular day, mentioned above, until shortly after I had successfully completed the grueling half-hour wait in the checkout line and was permitted to off-load the Himalayan mound of groceries I had selected onto the moving conveyor-belt. (Perhaps I should explain to my readers in Hominy Falls, West Virginia, where my last book did quite well and hopefully this one will too, who may not have such modern conveniences in *their* markets yet, that here in California, the very seat of technological sophistication, nowadays you have to unload all your own groceries onto the counter yourself; even fifty-pound bags of fertilizer, because this is called progress. Then the checkerperson drags each item carelessly over a piece of glass with a red light shining under it, and this complicated procedure causes an annoying dinging noise, and something presumably registers someplace. If there is no ding, the checkerperson slams your item back and forth again three or four times until it makes lots of dings and you get overcharged. That's how it works.)

Well, everything was going along miserably, as usual, and my huge pyramid of by now battered groceries, nearly all checked, double-checked or triple-checked, was in danger of toppling off the end of the counter, waiting for an elusive bagperson to decide to show up (checkerpersons don't do bags, if they can help it, because they have been promoted above all that menialness). Then, lo and behold, a bagperson put in an appearance and bagged everything in ten seconds flat and disappeared again before the final three items had been checked in. It was at this point that disaster struck, in the form of an innocent looking, one-quart jar of mayonnaise. The checkerperson, by then overdue for his coffee break, slammed the jar of mayonnaise across the glass. *DING!* $4,074.15! That's what the dang fool computer contraption demanded I

should pay for one lousy jar of mayonnaise. No way, José! I said I was swearing off mayonnaise for life. The checker-person said a colorful string of phrases that I don't think he learned in checkerperson training school and called the manager. The manager looked totally bewildered and said he'd have to go make a telephone call. The seven impatient souls behind me in line glared at me like I'd done something socially unacceptable. Meanwhile, my three half-gallons of ice cream (which I shouldn't have bought in the first place, in my condition) were slowly turning into warm milkshakes. Finally the manager returned, confessed that nothing like that had ever happened before, claimed that the fix-it man was on his way from Modesto and told me they would have to move me to another counter, un-bag everything and check out each item all over again. To pacify me, he sent the bagperson scurrying to get replacement ice cream. All this and still the experts maintain that computers are stupendous time and labor-saving devices, a boon to the modern world. BALDERDASH!

And you just can't escape the infernal gadgets and the chaos they cause. They've even invaded banks, once the recognized bastions of conservatism and math graduates. Of course I'll never know if the tellers in my bank ever took any math at all because, while they all seem to be very nice and we smile and nod at each other almost continuously during any transaction, not too many of them speak English, as we know it. This fact must make it more than a little difficult if a customer wants to do anything wildly outlandish, other than just deposit or withdraw. In fact, I thought there would be actual fisticuffs one day at the next teller-window over from me when a person with a strong German accent requested a money order from a Taiwanese teller. Neither could understand the other at all and soon the German lady, who was built a little like the *Hindenburg,* became so frustrated she started almost shouting her request. Frankly, it looked like she was gearing up to reach over and throttle the poor, cowering teller. So I quickly stepped over and interfered, as is often my habit, I guess, and printed a note in capital letters saying, "MONEY ORDER," and shoved it through the window at the startled bank employee. The teller, who undoubtedly had gone through specific training about what to do if a distraught person accosted her with a note, snatched it from my hand and went away somewhere, perhaps hunting for appropriate alarm buttons to push, and the customer grabbed me in a bear-hug in a show of Teutonic camaraderie and proceeded to yammer away in German, which I don't speak. Eventually an Iranian supervisor solved the problem, or at least I think he did. But I've wandered completely off the subject of computers, haven't I? As I get older this seems to be happening a lot.

You can always tell, almost immediately, when the computers are acting up in a bank. The tellers turn into zombies with long faces, like they've just had a lover's spat with their boyfriends, girlfriends, or whatever. You may have just brought in two checks, which you want deposited and posted in your bankbook, not something you would consider an insurmountable request in the financial world, but the employee sadly intones, "The computer is down." You glance around the room and notice at least twenty idle typewriters just sitting there doing nothing. Why, you ask yourself, can't they just do something simple like type the amount in my book and initial it, like they used to do in the olden days? But maybe the typewriters are staging a sympathy strike on behalf of the computers and when one's "down," they're all "down"? But that doesn't excuse all those ballpoint pens cluttering up the place. They're not plugged into anything. Have the tellers, even those who can't speak English, never been taught how to write down numbers? I sometimes feel I'm running loose in a world I no longer understand.

While we're on the subject, if one more person asks me if I do my writing on a computer, with a computer, or anywhere in the vicinity of a computer, word processor or whatever fancy name they call them, or suggests I can't possibly exist one more day without one, I'm apt to belt him or her right in the chops. It took me long enough just

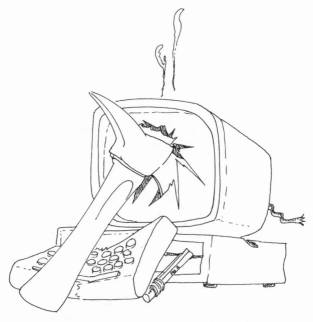

to get used to a typewriter that's no earthly good unless it's plugged in. I don't even have automatic shift on my car. How in the world could I ever hope to get the upper hand with a dad-blamed computer? It would know right away it was dealing with an idiot, go "down" and stay "down." Maybe we San Joseans are subjected to more of this electronic frenzy than others since we live here in what newcomers refer to as the "Silicon Valley" (I still think that first word refers to a substance you implant yourself with if you're still praying to get wolf whistles out of anyone, so I don't see why any sane person would be trying to promote it through their Chamber of Commerce, for heaven's sake). But they're full of it out here. In order to get along with those blasted hunks of machinery, one has to learn a whole new language, a language that's about as comprehensible as Swahili to most of us mature (over 55) genealogists. And you never quite know where one of these computer lunatics will pop up. I even came across one in the very last place you'd think of looking for that sort of specimen—Ohio!

I suppose if you fill a riverboat with a whole herd of genealogy speakers, many of whom were from highly cultivated places other than Ohio (not that I'm putting down that lovely state for a minute, you understand), along with the various groupies and hangers-on that cling to such speakers, you are simply not going to be able to escape coming up with at least one computer freak in the barrel. That's what happened with that Ohio River cruise which I discuss at infinitesimal length later in this book.

I had been herded on the boat by Joe and Jan, representatives of the publisher, who were stuck with trying to keep me entertained in Cincinnati, not an easy accomplishment for anyone, I've been told. Joe, a music buff, wanted to get closer to the source of the ear-splitting racket exploding out of the loudspeakers all over the boat. Jan just wanted to find a place to sit down and rest her throbbing feet, which she'd been standing on in high heels in the publisher's booth all day. I, on the other hand, wanted to partake of the one passionate pastime in which I always indulge when I find myself on a boat, and that is to climb to the uppermost deck, plant myself firmly on the front of it and watch the water go by, so as not to miss even a minute of it. Jan, declining my invitation to do the same, flung herself with rare abandon into the first available deck chair, slipped her shoes off and closed her eyes. Joe, not wanting to be burdened with an old bat all evening, looked around desperately for someone he could stick me with so that he could gracefully cut out. Along came what had to be one of the handsomest men on the boat (at least he looked like he still had his own teeth and wasn't wearing a toupee). And Joe acted like he knew him and may have even slipped him some money, for some reason. My heart fluttered a bit, which it hasn't forgotten entirely how to do. Here I was on a balmy night (balmy in Cincinnati in July is anytime the temperature is under 100 and they are not having thundershowers) with the full moon out so clear you could see it even without your bifocals, and I was propped up against the railing of a romantic riverboat, trying to act worldly and blasé and hoping I could somehow dredge up some fascinating topic of conversation to engage in with this hunk that would keep him hanging on every word for the whole two hours.

Do you know what he turned out to be? No, not a mad rapist, although perhaps one of them might have been easier to interact with. Out of that entire boatload of genealogicophiles, I wound up with probably the one and only *computeritzky*. Computers were his life, his universe, his whole reason for being, and he had gotten that way, for goodness sake, up in Minnesota or Wisconsin or one of those places where all they have is scenery, cows and snow. Why, I didn't realize they'd even discovered type-writers up there yet, much less computers. But it was this fellow's business and he was going around the country helping genealogy hobbyists do whatever it is they do with the infernal contraptions. I'm sure a goodly number of female genealogists wouldn't mind if he flopped his disks wherever he pleased.

If I ever do get mentally unstable enough (a pretty good possibility, now that I think of it) to get talked into pur-chasing a computer, I'm sure I'd mess it up somehow. But I guess even the experts can do that, from what I've heard. My good friend, Pat BOYD, at the local LDS Family History Center told me a horror story about one of their regular computer addicts. It seems he'd labored at his machine one whole day on a very long and complicated chart of Welsh surnames. Finally, late that night, with the golden glow of accomplishment on his brow, thoroughly exhausted but rightfully proud of his newly-created, mas-sive list, he leaned back in his chair to survey his master-piece. In doing so, his feet caught on the electric cord and pulled out the plug, sending his creation straight to obliv-ion. So much for computers.

Now that I've imputted my output to the maximum and can't dig up anything else compatible about this whole electronic nightmare of a subject, you can just play around with your blooming software to your heart's content and I'm going to climb out of this alien territory and move on to something I can recognize—people, herds of people.

> *"A man who prides himself on his ancestry is like the potato plant, the best part of which is underground."* — Spanish Proverb

Will the D.O.O.D.O.O. Replace the D.A.R.?

Caution: This chapter is meant only for the eyes of you genealogy hobbyists who are members of the *haut monde* or some other mound of rigid gentility, for those of you who recognize the pressing need to belong, and for those of you who have been soundly rejected by the D.A.R., the S.A.R., the C.A.R., the D.F.P., the S.M.D., the D.A.C. and the P.D.Q. What I'm doing here is plunking down before you a brilliant proposal for the immediate establishment of a brand-new genealogical society, because Lord knows there is certainly a crying need for more of them. Come to think of it, you had better make that *two* new societies. You have to have a separate one for men, even in this age of liberation. Otherwise they'll come to yours and smoke and try to take over. Now, as you know, membership in the first three organizations above is based on ironclad, sworn-to-in-a-blood-oath proof of your downward connection to the earthly remains of anything from a celebrated military hero to some poor ignorant

farmer who just happened to find himself in the wrong
place with his musket and got caught in a skirmish, just
so long as it all happened over 200 years ago back East.
Actually, it didn't even have to be strictly military. You
could even qualify if you were descended from some
female who may have been following the military men
around, performing necessary functions, so long as she
was patriotic.

But we now face a serious problem in that regard, at
least in the D.A.R., the S.A.R. and the C.A.R., because
we have simply exhausted ourselves honoring everyone
thirty times over who ever rode his, or her, horse to within
shooting distance of a Revolutionary War battlefield.
We've done run out, so to speak. Therefore it becomes our
bounden duty to select another category to deify. Now,
even though there is a society connected with it, no one
remembers much about the War of 1812, perhaps because
there hasn't been a television mini-series on that one yet,
so we can skip right over it as being too inconsequential
to form another society about. That way we need not fret
needlessly about the possibility of conflicting initials.
Instead, let's move on to that highly popular, romantic
escapade we now call the Civil War. (In the North, at the
time, it was actually called The Rebellion, and the rash
Dixieites probably referred to it as The Fight For Freedom, but we'll just chuck all those provincial designations
out once and for all.) If we were to form a new society
connected with expired folks who fought in that war, we
could schedule special balls and celebrations where we
ladies could get to wear hoopskirts and snoods and say
"I do declare" and "y'all" a lot and practice making kit-
tenish moues like Scarlett O'HARA. The men members
could wear those cute little stylish blue or grey kepis and
try to figure out how to get the rust off their cannons. But,

on second thought, I suppose a society of this nature is doomed to failure from a national standpoint, because it is *de rigueur* to have national conventions, as everyone knows, and if you were to try something like that when you have hot-heads from Georgia, Alabama, Pennsylvania and New York all in the same room, why, sure as shooting, that's exactly what we'd probably be doing all over again. No, we'd better play it safe and try for a certain blandness.

Heaven knows, we have oodles of other wars to choose from, but they are either too recent to suggest much imaginative pageantry, or they're lost in obscurity. We certainly don't want to fool around with the War in Vietnam. Most of us are much too old and out of shape to tackle a rampaging Jane FONDA at this point in our lives. But wait a minute here. When you come right down to it there is no Marquess of Queensberry rule that says we have to base a new society on persons who fought in an actual *war*. If the only requirement they had to have was the inability to get along with someone else, well then I have a great suggestion. One trait many of our ancestors did have in common, whether they were upstanding Unionists or despicable Confederates, whether they high-tailed it out of merry old England on the *Mayflower,* or have barely dried out their serapes after a midnight swim across the Rio Grande, is that a great number of them (many more than ever fought in the Revolution, by the way, so we'd be in no danger of running out) learned the uncomplicated art of breaking the law. Our founding fathers couldn't get along with the British; criminals can't get along with the law. *Voilà!*

Lest some of you shriek with horror, take immediate umbrage and go into an absolute state of shock that anyone should dare put forth the idea of glorifying lawbreakers, heaven help us all, please stop for a minute and think about it. Our brave patriots of the Revolutionary War were not only breaking the law too, they were consummate traitors if you were looking at them from the other side of the ocean. You see, it's all relative. The one selling point that my plan has going for it is that horse thieves, and others of their ilk, got plenty written down about them all over the place. Like *recorded records*. Now do you get it? There is a nearly virgin treasure trove of untapped records and information just sitting and waiting to be violated in the Circuit Courts of America. It wouldn't be nearly as frustrating as trying to prove your dear ancestor stood right there side-by-side with General WASHINGTON when CORNWALLIS poutingly handed over his sword. Indictments don't pussy-foot around. They name names!

On the other hand, just think how frustrating it would be trying to set up a society of descendants of plain old honest (or nearly so) businessmen, merchants, or other workers. But, in all fairness, I did hear of a happy bunch who call themselves the Daughters of Colonial Tavern Keepers and I'd sure be willing to drink to that one. I can just imagine where they hold their meetings and in what state they have to be to attend them. And how in the world do they keep the men out? As to other possible occupations to choose from, what do you do if your forebears were simple farmers (ho hum), lamplighters or blacksmiths? Those poor dudes just did what they did and didn't waste quill pen and ink writing down every blessed, dreary detail of how they did it so that they could hop on old Nellie and gallop down to the nearest courthouse and try to get it recorded. The best P.I. in the business couldn't track down those fellows. No, your average pioneer good citizen in the olden days, unless all he did all day was whittle, avoided the courthouses just as religiously as we do today, not wanting to get stuck with serving on a jury or to get cornered by a long-winded politician running for office, not when he (the citizen) should be home planting crops or, better still, impregnating his wife (or someone else's).

Nobody knew or cared what most folks were up to in times past. If you were lucky enough to survive infancy, you spent your short childhood trying to stay out of the way of your father's razor strop. Then, when you were considered growed up, usually well before ten years of age, you worked. At the end, you died. That was it. The government was not yet doling out large sums of the tax-payers' money for expensive studies of every infinitesimal happening of everyday life so that they could then persuade you to stop smoking, making love, and eating anything that tastes good. If your ancestors saw a rat or mouse, they just dispatched it promptly with a broom, pitchfork or shotgun. They didn't carry it off to a labora-

tory, stuff it full of forty pounds of one kind of substance and wonder why it dropped dead. If a house painter expired of the usual lead poisoning before he could finish painting your gazebo, well you just went out and got yourself another painter. Nobody worried about it much. After all, those were the good old days.

The point I'm trying to make is that not an awful lot was put down in black-and-white about people in most occupations. And the whole thrust of the hobby of genealogy is that you are expected to accumulate tons and tons of copies of records about individuals who did things that got mentioned somehow in writing and that same writing got saved somehow. At least we are lucky enough to be participating in the hobby at the present time. Traditionally, letter writing, journal keeping, diary filling and all other forms of written expression were considered a worthwhile and genteel way of spending one's time in years gone by. Pity the poor genealogy nut of the future trying to locate ancestors living in our own time when everything is on computers and records can be erased forever at the pull of a plug! In this day and age even those who have no access to a computer wouldn't be caught dead, if you'll pardon the expression, actually sitting around writing anything down. I mean, it ain't in, man. We've almost progressed back to the Stone Age, when you think about it.

But what, you ask, can we call our illustrious new societies? They have to have full, formal names so that they can forevermore be known by their initials only. We could call one "Daughters of Old Offenders, Desperados and Other Outlaws," or D.O.O.D.O.O., and the other one S.C.A.T., "Sons of Criminals, Assassins and Thugs." That would go well in my local county where the brilliant elected officials actually chose the latter set of initials with which to christen our spanking new trolley system. When the laughter died down, somebody patiently sat down with

the said puzzled officials and wrote out a program on a floppy disk explaining a few well-known biological facts about the animal kingdom and its phraseology. I'm not sure they completely understand it yet, being city-bred, but they eventually voted to change the name to something worse that starts with an "F".

If there are no men interested in the hobby in your home town, you could just use one name, shortened so that you could fit it on your stationery better. Something like "Daughters of Dead Offenders," or D.O.D.O., would be nice and snappy. Whatever you decide to call yourselves, you should be able to use up two or three entire meetings arguing about a name if you work things right. So as to not waste too much time in the planning stages, however, you could just lift the Rules and Regulations and By-Laws from some other society (lifting should be quite in keeping with the hereditary propensities of your proposed new members, don't you think?). Then you could go on to add some special incentives to really personalize your organization, like a red star behind your name on the membership roll for every individual offense you can find an indictment for in your family tree. That sort of honor should certainly spur everyone on to a frenzy of fresh research. Or you could have different colored stars for different types of offenses. As you can see, there are endless possibilities.

I've been asked how the timid researcher could ever get up enough courage to approach a county clerk with a request to see the criminal records. Just remember, the first time is always the hardest. By a stroke of good luck, my initial experience in this regard was an unplanned one and occurred while working on my husband's family. Luckier still, we were toiling away in a great county for genealogical research, Vermillion County, Indiana where, at that time anyway, they just turned you loose in the room where they kept the dusty, heavy old books and let you pull down any volume or file box you could reach, even if you had to climb up the rickety ladder to fetch it. (Warning: Their rules may have changed by now.) We were beginners to the hobby that year and had almost no idea that one book was any different from another. We knew that the intelligent hobbyist was encouraged to procure copies of birth certificates, marriage records, death certificates and wills. We did overhear someone else in the room ask for land records but we mistakenly assumed him to be a lawyer, a person who naturally gravitates toward the very dullest of reading matter. We didn't realize until later that genealogy hobbyists' tastes run in the same direction.

In order to understand what a bombshell we later uncovered in that courthouse on that day, it is necessary to paint a brief word-picture about my husband's family. Permit me to explain that they are conservative. *Boy, are they conservative!!!* To this day, they don't even recognize the word "Democrat" or anything it stands for. Back in the Civil War, Alan's grandfather's company of Indiana volunteer infantry was known as "The Preachers' Regiment," and it was rumored that their idea of a wild, devil-may-care time was to sit around the campfire and sing hymns and sip lukewarm apple cider. WOWEE!!! And there's still a lot of that degree of Indiana excitability recognizable in the descendants who live out here in Sodom and Gomorrah West (California), impossible as that may be to believe. They'd sooner resign from the human race than break the law in any way whatsoever. You can't even get them to jaywalk, for goodness sake.

So, now to our discovery in the courthouse . . . The hours passed happily by while we got grubbier and grubbier, turning the pages thick with dust, uncovering neat, circumspect marriages, deaths from dull and proper causes, and wills with few surprises, all prim, in order, and par for the course, considering the utmost propriety of that particular family. After we had spent most of the morning so occupied, and as I was close to dozing off from lack of excitement, I pulled down a volume from a slightly different location on the shelves and noticed that it was labeled "Circuit Court Cases." Eureka! Guess what I found? An old court order, stating in formal, legal language that the local sheriff was thereby charged with going forth and "bringing in the body" (still living) forthwith of one of Alan's family members who had been (horror of horrors!) *gambling* by tossing coins for "spirits and crackers" (the poor fellow was probably just hungry and thirsty, who knows?). The stakes in his case were pretty high, in those days, amounting to 25¢ a toss, and he seemed to be unfairly trying to enhance his odds of winning by brandishing a firearm which he was apparently using as a bit of a persuader. From a later record we

learned that when the sheriff sallied forth to do his duty, the renegade in question politely declined to come back to jail and backed up his obstinacy with his pistol. Of course, my husband, equally obstinate, staunchly refused to believe that such a ruffian, even if his name was clearly **MOORE**, had any connection whatsoever with his upstanding folks of the same name, and he still insists the rascal was using a pseudonym. I just laughed and laughed and kept pointing out other recorded violations for the same chap, all for participating in ingenious games of chance, undoubtedly frowned upon with horror at that time (and perhaps still, for all I know) as unacceptable behavior in a location which was not exactly known as a wide-open state full of heathenish activities, not by a long shot.

In some counties you may have a struggle on your hands trying to pry the circuit court records off the shelves in the hallowed sanctuaries where they are kept. At the very least, you may get static from the keepers of the records. It took me a good quarter of an hour in one courthouse cajoling the female employees who labored there (as little as possible) that I really was dead serious about wanting to see the old books containing criminal court cases. One young lady, convinced that she was dealing with a squirrelly old broad who had more than a few screws loose, kept saying, "But, Ma'am, your family couldn't possibly be in *those* books." "Oh yes, they could," said I, equally insistent, "and probably a lot more often than you can imagine, Miss." She finally realized that the only way she would get me to go away was to show me one of the books, offer me a table and chair, and let me see for myself that she was right and that I was subjecting them to a very foolish request indeed. Three hours later, while I was still busily Xeroxing "fresh" old criminal records, the same bewildered clerk was mumbling, "I can't believe it. I can't believe it." (She just didn't know my family like I did.) The "U" indexes in that county had more court cases listed for my UNDERWOODs than cases headed "United States of America," of which there were many. My husband was laughing so hard by that time, he had to ask the lady for directions to the men's room.

Amongst the cases you look at, when doing a search of this type, are those considered more scandalous in nature than criminal. Take the one which, I suspect, caused my husband to lose control. It seemed that one of my more hot-blooded kin, and a female he knew (in the Biblical sense), were slapped with an adultery charge. They were caught with their pants down, in the literal sense, but "failed to appear" for their subsequent trial, according to the tale left for posterity in the formal old casebook. They were found guilty anyway. I think they showed surprisingly good judgment, not putting in an appearance, considering the outcome. He would have been rewarded by being placed at hard labor on the public highways and she would have been thrown in the slammer. I'd light out too, if I had my druthers, wouldn't you?

The greatest thing about checking out your family in the criminal records is that, if they were really inventive and diversified in their activities, your research could turn up a whole lot more colorful information than you ever found in the stodgy old Births, Marriages, Deaths, Wills and Estate Settlement books you spent so much time perusing. You may even learn terms you may not have

been familiar with before. For instance, I wondered about the peculiar charge filed against one of the female members of my family, which was given as "Maintaining a Nuisance." (???) Once he'd gotten over another rude fit of laughter, my exasperating husband, who has a law degree and understands big words, explained that the lady (?) had opened up her private residential establishment and taken in paying guests, of a sort, in keeping with what was probably her only means of livelihood. Harumph! What was wrong with that, I wondered?

Another charge that puzzled me was one brought against a single, solitary male relative. It was for "Confederating and Banding Together." How, in all that's sane, could one man do that all by himself? Probably what it was is that the local deputies just got a little overly nervous when they spotted one of my kin hanging around town, looking idle, and they decided not to take any chances. A number of other charges were for "being of unsound mind." (???) Since when is that an offense?

So you see what a rollicking good time you can have if you decide to form a clique devoted to exposing all those juicy and scandalous tidbits thought to be safely hidden away in the circuit court files all these years. Say, you might even be able to finance your whole organization if you uncover the wrong sort of thing about the right sort of person right there in your own home town.

Now, whether your ancestors were heroes of the bloody Revolution, refugees of the potato famine, or businesswomen of the streets, and no matter how many of their high jinks were written down for posterity, don't you sometimes wish they would have made an appointment with Mathew BRADY, or some other fellow with a photography salon, and had their pictures taken? It's one thing to wonder if everyone hanging in your family tree had that same sort of simian look that marks the modern-day members, but it's quite another thing to see the proof for yourself.

Curses!
An Unidentified
Photograph!

Along with the continuing frenzy of unearthing "new" written records and information as you hobble around from this library to that research center, I sincerely hope each and every one of you will enjoy the ultimate of electrifying experiences, that of actually holding in your own trembling hands photographic representations of your dearly departed predecessors. Seeing that sort of thing should make the juices rise right up in your gorge and overwhelm you. It might even answer some of the questions you've had for so many years, like why is there a family tendency toward moustaches (on the females, that is), or ears that flop out at right angles, or eyes that appear to be set closer together than other people's. All the familiar little idiosyncrasies looking back at you in the mirror every morning had to come from somewhere, you tell yourself, and pictures may just solve the mystery quicker than anything.

For the first five years of my own research, unfortu-

— UNCLE NED —

nately even after I'd gone to such lengths as publishing my own family history, I'd suffered an absolute drought as far as old photographs were concerned. I mean, talk about deprived, I didn't even have any early pictures of my father and mother, much less of anyone dangling any further back on my family tree. I was pea-green with envy at all the other genealogists I knew because, almost without exception, they were the proud possessors of lovely old-fashioned, stern portraits of their dignified forebears, which they were forever pompously flashing around, and I had none. You know the kind of pictures I'm referring to, the ones where no one is ever smiling (when you get a load of the constricting clothing they were wearing, you can see why they weren't) and where the subjects were seated stiffly upright or were standing like they had a pole up their bustle (in some cases, I understand, they literally did—to keep them still).

But back to my problem . . . I was convinced that my mother had scads of old pictures because I clearly remembered spending hours on rainy days howling with laughter over them as a child, too ignorant to know how terribly important they would become to me one day. Since Mother never believed in giving away or (heaven forbid!) throwing away a single, solitary item ever, I was reasonably sure that they were still buried somewhere in her hopelessly cluttered house. I began to use every occasion imaginable to drop none-too-subtle hints. Finally I outright asked. But she wasn't the least bit interested in genealogy and informed me that she had no intention of trying to burrow down and locate anything as useless as old photograph albums, and that was simply the end of the subject as far as she was concerned. Well, since Mother

had regularly announced to the family that she fully intended to live to the year 2000 at least (and I've always had equally strong feelings that I never would), I allowed as how I'd best give up on ever making contact with the family pictures. Then, three years ago, the Hand that writes the scenes for all of us to follow stepped in and dealt Mother a none-too-happy blow in the form of Alzheimer's Disease. It then became my duty to care for her and begin the massive cleanup of her huge two-story house. As you can imagine, it was a little like Lord CARNARVON turning Howard CARTER loose in the Valley of the Kings, like nominating a fox to be superintendent of the hen-house. The excavating began with a vehemence and I'm not finished yet. I'm still uncovering treasures in the form of faded letters, pictures, newspaper articles, journals, and other keepsakes of an earlier time. But I'll never forget the first one that I found. It was Mother's parents' delicate ivory-trimmed Hungarian family Bible, and out of the ancient pages fluttered a formal studio portrait of her family, taken in late 1905 in Cleveland, Ohio. At long last I had my own dignified family portrait to show to everybody and brag about. As you can see, my mother is a tiny babe-in-arms and she appears to be the only one in the picture who isn't drunk as a skunk. She's being held by my grandfather, who has an even tighter grip on a bottle of wine. Not to be outdone, my grandmother, tilted at an odd angle up against a table, is lifting a full stein of beer to her lips. Her glassy-eyed sister-in-law is not only tippling but, for some reason, has a rifle slung over her shoulder. Now, please understand, this was the serious, peace-loving branch of my family, so I can't imagine what was going on. Was this considered fashionable behavior in the better photography salons in Cleveland in those days? Or, could this have been the traditional Hungarian way of celebrating a christening? But I shouldn't complain. It beats having no picture at all.

So, to those of you hobbyists who find yourselves barren of pictures, I can only advise you to be patient. Someone out there somewhere may have pictures of your early family members, even if it's only on an old "wanted" bill. Keep looking, for the odds might someday favor you with a windfall.

Now, as bad as it is to have no pictorial mementos at all, there is yet another vexation which may even cause more gnashing of dentures. How many of you rabid genealogists are wallowing around in scores and scores of lovely old portraits in near-perfect condition, none of which bears a clue as to who it is? The unidentified photograph is the bane of the otherwise cheerful genealogy hobbyist. Who could it be? Who is there left to ask? Why didn't the blooming dunderheads write down the identity, or identities, and the date, for God's sake, on the back? How could they have been so stupid? But wait a blithering minute here. Would you like to check the pictures you yourself have taken of your own little family and friends, meticulously snapped ever since you've been old enough to learn how to operate a camera? Are they all identified? Of course not, you say, that's silly, I *know* who all the people are in *my* pictures. Uh, huh. You see how it happens?

A crystal clear example of the frustration which can grab you by the throat when you find yourself in a confrontation with unidentified photographs hit me last year. While cleaning a basement closet in Mother's house, I came across two big cardboard boxes full of mice droppings, mildew, spiders, and old studio portraits. After hours of impatient cleaning, it became clear to me that I hadn't the foggiest notion whose pictures they were. Sure, they were in the possession of my mother, but she had had a bunch of husbands and filched souvenirs from each of them, so how was I supposed to know from what line these pictures had sprung? I certainly couldn't expect Mother to identify them. We're lucky when she can identify me these days, much less anything else around her. Luckily, underneath the photographs in one box were letters and newspaper clippings which all seemed to have some connection to various persons named BURNSIDE. So I made the scholarly deduction that the pictures must be BURNSIDEs too. It was then that the discovery of those two boxes of treasures started preying on my mind (what's left of it) until it has become an absolute obsession. You see, I'm not a BURNSIDE. That was my stepfather's name. I don't even know any BURNSIDEs. I'm beginning to think there was a curse in those boxes. Those dad-blamed unidentified BURNSIDEs are burning a hole in my file cabinet and driving me bonkers. I keep imagining that if someone had found two boxes of photographs of my GALEENERs, lovely, sharp pictures, some of them dating back to before the Civil War, I would kill to get my hands on that kind of a jackpot. Those !@#$%¢&*() pictures have become such a fixation that I swear they are haunting me. I've started spending my spare time and money researching a consarned surname that isn't even on my family chart, not biologically at any rate. But I can almost visualize that dramatic moment somewhere in the future when someone will step out of the fog, à la STANLEY and LIVINGSTONE, and I'll say, "BURNSIDE, I presume?" and unload those blankety-blank pictures on their rightful blood-relative.

You know, I hesitated to do a chapter about photography because, quite frankly, if you were to ask for my credentials on the subject, it is entirely possible that I would come up a tiny bit lacking. I'll have to admit, the first time my husband ever actually handed over our camera for me to operate, the result would have been a really close closeup of my right eyeball, due, I suppose, to what your so-called camera fanatics might refer to as reverse projection. After someone told me to turn it around I don't recollect that the results were much improved. Years later, when I finally found myself in control once again of another camera, I probably would have had thirty-six of the best, most detailed snapshots of the intricate pattern of the inside of the lens cover ever taken, if they had just come out. So, if it's professional expertise you're expecting, you're in the wrong pew. But I can sure tell you how *not* to do it.

Whether you are prepared for it or not, fellow genealogists, you may be forced to get familiar with how to take

pictures. Over and above the thousands of breath-taking
shots you'll want to take of such things as half-toppled
gravestones, clusters of living relatives with arms entwined
squinting myopically into the lens, and those various spots
of bare ground where you think your great-grandfather's
house may have stood maybe, you might find another use
for your busy camera, one that could give you a little help
in stretching the old genealogy budget. I'm talking about
the frugal practice of taking your own pictures of pictures.
Otherwise, if you were to inherit a really neat old portrait
of your Uncle Gloud and your Aunt Zephiniah and their
fifteen solemn offspring, how in the world are you going
to share it with other family members who demand a piece
of the action? I came face to face with reality in one fell
swoop recently when I naively wandered into a local photography salon and asked the price they would charge to
copy a precious boyhood picture of my father I had found.
After recovering from shock, I beat a hasty retreat with
my wallet intact and vowed to forevermore use the sensi-

ble approach—ask my husband to do it. Believe me, you'll pay through the nose otherwise.

I broached this very problem some months ago to a very dear friend of mine, Pat BOYD, a knowledgeable volunteer at the local LDS Family History Center and, therefore, more than qualified to deal with all levels of stupidity. As luck would have it, Pat was becoming an expert with the camera, mainly in self defense, after coming into possession of a treasure trove of pictures and memorabilia she'd lifted from her mother's house in much the same circumstances as I had from mine. She claimed it would be simple to teach me how to take pictures of pictures (not being aware, I guess, of my record as a photographer). To start, she introduced me to three little black gizmos you are supposed to screw on the camera someplace (once you figure out in a highly professional manner which side of the blasted instrument to aim away from your body). After I had become thoroughly familiar with the three whatchamacallits, she said we had to go do it outside for some reason connected with daylight, so she led the way out to the parking lot behind the research facility, thereby frightening off a handful of startled hoodlums who were busy acquiring their daily supply of hubcaps and other selected auto parts. Next, Pat picked out a plain grey car that belonged to someone she knew (so we wouldn't get yelled at), spread some snow-white toweling on the car's hood and told me to put my pictures on the toweling. At this point, she went into a complicated discourse about how it was most important that I remember that the sun had to be in a certain spot relative to the pictures and how a person should only attempt this procedure at certain exact times of day, or it would get all screwed up and you would get a glare or shadows or something bad, only I forget what. She also patiently explained the use of each of the three deelybobs and just what reason a photographer would have to use each of them, or some of them, or all of them, I think. After she did all the explaining that she figured might have a chance of catching hold, she performed various acrobatics over the acquiescent pictures, snapping two or three shots of each like the professionals do. When she was finished she asked, "Now do you understand it all?" One look at my face, which must have been displaying the customary amount of blankness when anything too mechanically technical creeps into the conversation, and Pat gave up and wrote it all down in a little note for me to take home to my husband.

Alan had no trouble deciphering the note so we are now the proud possessors of our own set of three little black gizmos and have begun making stacks and stacks of pictures of pictures, just in case. You can never tell when someone in our family might get a craving for one or two of them, so it's best to be prepared. If your family is like ours, however, you'll find that visiting relatives tend to yawn a lot or, if you're really lucky, they suddenly remember reasons why they have to leave for somewhere else when you drag out the pile of pictures, so this useful pastime can be a boon to you in ways you never expected. Someday, of course, you should remember to jot down the identification and approximate original date on each picture, but for now, if you have storage space problems, you can just stick them in cardboard boxes and put them down in the basement for safekeeping.

Now that I've bestowed such a vast wealth of intricate, precise directions on you so as to enable you to practically become Photographer Laureate of your genealogical society, we should really wade back into the red meat of genealogy, the actual research. This is a relatively easy accomplishment if your ancestors had the good sense to come from a country that speaks the American language, and it's especially convenient, whether they forked over their hard-earned shillings for a voluntary trip on a three-master, or manned the fifth oar on the left down in the galley while fashionably attired in chains, that they did it as early as possible. Heaven help those of you who have foreigners for ancestors!

> *"Whenever the literary German dives into a sentence, that is the last you are going to see of him till he emerges on the other side of his Atlantic with his verb in his mouth."* — Mark TWAIN

So Your BODENSCHATZ Came from Rügenwaldermündenbergerfurt?

Of all the impossible places my Hungarian SPONDER grandfather had to pick to come from, Hungary was probably the worst. Why, far be it from me to point an accusing finger, but I'll lay you odds that back in those pre-World War One days, as near as I can figure, those armies rampaging around back there had to have been dipping in and skimming a hefty kickback from right off the top of the profit margin of the European map makers' earnings. How else can you explain why those boundaries were in perpetual motion in that neck of the woods? Of course, their tendency to sprinkle paprika on everything and to drink the type of wine that would disintegrate pig-iron might have made them a tad more restless than, say, the Swedes, for instance, but can you think of what problems this antsyness must have caused? School children in Grandfather's old neighborhood must have had a deuce of a time remembering the Pledge of Allegiance each morning when they couldn't even tell what country they were in

67

that day. I've found my grandfather's father not only officially listed as Hungarian, but also Austrian, Polish, Ger-

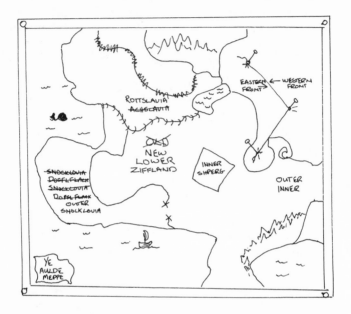

man and Czechoslovakian. (???) It must have been pure
hell to try to memorize the heads of state when the name
of the state itself could change quicker than you could say
"Franz Joseph." And they not only shuffled the boundaries around with great frequency, but they also changed
the names of burgs, évszaks, provinces and anything else
they could march through just about as often, so you
never knew at the end of a long day out behind your ox
tilling the fields whether your village would even be there
when you got home. I suspect their mail delivery must
have been frightful, almost in as confused a state as our
modern service is today. And maybe even the army had
trouble keeping track of the daily situation. If you were a
Hussar sporting a bright red shako on your head when you

reported for reveille, by sundown you were probably under orders to run your sword through anyone caught wearing a bright red shako. When you think of it, it's not a bit surprising that the more laid-back Austrians or Serbians or whatever they were, chose to spend their time creating whipped-cream desserts or waltzes or something with more permanence.

What's amazing to me is that, in amongst all this absolute chaos, they managed to do a pretty good job of writing down the records which are important to us as genealogy hobbyists, even though they never seemed to have found anyone bright enough to write them down in English. I've spent years trying to find my Hungarian grandfather's birth record. I am pretty sure I have the correct date and place, 21 June 1866 in Budapest. Every time I go on a hunting expedition to Salt Lake City I request more Hungarian films to be brought up from the vaults (they have so many of them that I don't think I have enough years left to see them all). I've probably sat still through 172 entire reels of that specific time period by now, until I can tell the kereszteléseks from the házasságoks at the drop of a gyümölcsfa, so to speak, and I still haven't found his bloody birth record. I haven't even found any SPONDER at all doing anything worth recording for twenty years on either side of that date. On the outside chance that Grandfather had secretly decided to adopt an alias once he cut loose from the Old Country (which wouldn't have been such a bad idea considering he was leaving a wife and family behind), I even started checking for any male baby named Stephen (well, not technically Stephen because those dad-blasted Hungarian/Austrian/Slovaks couldn't seem to spell it correctly; the best they could do was István or Pista or Hey You), but nothing seemed to match. A native Hungarian I once met laughingly told me that SPONDER isn't even an Hungarian surname, so now what do I do? I suppose I will just keep on wasting my time, and the patience of the kind volunteers back in Salt Lake City, even though the chances of my ever finding that confounded birth record are about as good as coming across an icicle in Death Valley in July.

On the other hand, doing research on my maternal Hungarian grandmother was a snap. Even though Grandfather used to call her a !@#$%¢&*() peasant, by golly, her family left records! What took a little doing, however, was finding out where they left them. But then I remembered. If Grandmother said it once, she must have said it 99,786,435,283 times (in my hearing anyway) that her family came from a little place in Hungary called Horvaty. Of course, recognizing the good old Hungarian penchant for disorder, I hardly expected to find it still going by that name, or even to be still located in that country, as we now know it. Since Grandfather was also quoted as lovingly referring to Grandmother as an ignorant Slovak, I reckoned it might be worthwhile to start with Czechoslovakia. Now, to check out Czechs, if you'll pardon a pun, one must conduct oneself properly and submit all requests through the lone recognized channel for that sort of activity, the Czechoslovakian Embassy or Consulate, the official red-Czechers. And don't let the fact that they are dedicated communists fool you. They aren't the least bit shy asking for filthy capitalist shekels for their efforts on your behalf. In fact, be prepared to pony up a goodly bit of lucre before they will ever consent to part with a record. Once I managed to scrape together the money (by claiming it would be in lieu of a Christmas gift for the next five years), the Czechs did keep their end of the bargain and forwarded six generations of Grandmother's family tree (on paper, not in person). The only remaining question I could think of to ask them at that point was to pinpoint the present location of Horvaty, which they quaintly spelled Chorváty, in keeping with a policy of confusion. They never did answer that final question but then maybe they couldn't find it either. Later, a helpful volunteer in Salt Lake City found two of them, Horvatys I mean, so perhaps that was the problem. They were in Nová Bodva and Tupá (take your pick), neither one of which sounds like the kind of hot tourist spot I'd care to visit.

As materialistic as Czechoslovakia can be, France is simply one big pain in the patoot, as far as my research there has gone. Unfortunately, the first person on my paternal GALEENER branch to wise up and head for America was a Frenchman who, we've all been told, fought in the American Revolution (presumably on our side, although I'm not taking any bets). It sounded like he should be a simple enough dude to track down, so I optimistically jumped headfirst into the search and aimed for the horse's main part, France. Before long, some kind soul warned me that modern-day Frenchmen (and French women, too, for that matter) have an annoying preference for being addressed in French (danged persnickety of them, by God!) Well, I hate to admit it, but about all I know in French is "oui" and "nyet," and stuff like that, so I was forced to lean on two of our daughters, using the threat of disinheritance to get them to "voluntarily" come to my aid. I sent the letter that they grumblingly composed, thoroughly Frenchified, and accompanied by double the required return reply coupons (in a little attempt at bribery so that I'd hopefully receive an answer) off to Paris. Then I began hovering in the bushes around my mailbox, waiting for some kind of a speedy bonanza of information in return. What I got, two months later, was what appeared to be a list, as near as I could tell (it being all in French, wouldn't you know), of either people, libraries, wine names or French pastries, I wasn't sure. When I cornered a daughter, she finally confessed that there were professional researchers' names on the list, even though she realized that such an admission would only result in her being pestered into writing another French letter. She was right.

The next letter we received, I was informed, demanded a healthy fee in advance and was personally signed by some Frenchman, giving his title as "Voleur de Grand Chemin." So I sent him money and another generous offering of return reply coupons. Months later his "report" arrived. In it, my daughter translated, he proudly announced that he had found the exact name I had sent to him in the exact book where I told him it could be found. Other than that, he added, he had not found any other information anywhere about that particular person either before or after he was listed as sailing to America. Down at the bottom of the page, almost as an afterthought, he mentioned that there was a lengthy manuscript dealing with that specific surname and dating back to the Middle Ages in the national library. But he chose not to confide in me as to what it contained. Well, you know from your own experience that this kind of a juicy morsel can practically get you slavering at the mouth, so I badgered my poor daughter to do a rush-job on another missive to Paris, just a very brief one this time, asking how much he wanted to send along some kind of a clue as to what was in the manuscript. Seven years later I'm still waiting for his answer. Phooey on French research!

Understandably, the last time I was in Salt Lake City I raced to the European floor of the LDS Family History Library, only to see the notice behind the French expert's name indicating that he was "en vaginaux" or "en vacance," or anyway he was off somewhere. A German expert tried to help me the best he could with my French problem but it's just not the same. I think there's too much inborn friction there, or something. He did come up with a book with French surnames in it that someone had hidden behind the desk, so he was on the right track. Maybe next year . . .

Then there's my husband, who's been rather discouraged about his own research lately, having been burdened from birth with the frightfully plebian surname MOORE, which is almost on a par with JONES and SMITH. He has never tried to do much with his maternal BODEN-SCHATZ side, even though that's a name you can really sink your teeth into. It doesn't take too much deductive reasoning to guess what country spawned that name. In fact, that particular branch of Alan's family was so violently German, and so recently arrived from there, that I can still remember the oldest uncle, who'd actually been born in Der Vaterland, practically having a hemorrhage the day Alan brought some kind of a hybrid Hungarian/ French mongrel (me) into the family.

So, with an eye toward goosing my husband into getting actively engaged again in genealogy (with the sneaky, hidden hope that I might have an easier time talking him into a European vacation that way), I decided it was time for him to launch himself into the world of German research, whether he wanted to or not. The best way, of course, would be for me to make the magnanimous gesture of initiating the research for him. Then maybe he'd cave in. Accordingly, the next time I found myself in Milwaukee I joined a national German genealogical society, whose officers happened to be there, sampling the suds. (I'd always heard it wasn't difficult to find a German connection in Milwaukee, and quite often even sober ones at that.)

One thing I've learned in the year since I joined is that German genealogical societies are all business (the monkeying around in Milwaukee notwithstanding). They don't feature frivolity in their newsletter at all. Instead, it has a formal eagle in bold black print under the title to put you on guard (Germans have had a hangup about eagles for some time, as I recall), and some of the columns are appropriately headed "ACHTUNG!" And I have a sneaking suspicion that the editor wears shiny black boots, even when he sits at his desk. Not surprisingly, there are a lot of German words in the newsletter, leading one to guess that someone down there in Los Angeles, where they have their schlosseinfamilienforschung, probably speaks German. All members are ordered to send in their German surnames, and I suppose I could have gone ahead and taken a chance on SPONDER, for goodness sake, because my grandfather had as much chance of being German as of being anything else, but then I would have had to confess his sin of being born in Budapest (maybe), and such an admission would probably have resulted in storm troopers knocking on my front door in the dead of night. So I cheated and submitted good old safe BODEN-SCHATZ. As luck would have it, Field Marshal HINDENBURG, once President of Germany, was blessed with BODENSCHATZs in his tree, so I'm in like FLYNN, I think. And now I know what to get Alan for Christmas, one of those snazzy little helmets with a spike on top, something he can wear to the office. Somehow, the titillating news that he might just be related to the guy who sold out Germany to HITLER hasn't motivated Alan much. I can't understand why?

Speaking of the German society, the latest issue of their newsletter just this minute arrived in the mail, eagles and

all. Once again, browsing through it, I find myself more than a little intimidated by the query page. No, it isn't so much the queries that have me scared off, I can be pretty blasé about them since they've never been concerned with any surnames I've ever heard of. It's the instructions at the top of the page that have me quaking, and it's not likely they'll ever get a query out of me because I doubt that I have the advanced technical knowledge necessary to figure out what in the Sam Hill they're talking about. Among myriad complicated instructions, the query submitter is required to use secret German symbols, known only to those few pack-rat members who still have in their possession a certain year-old back issue of the newsletter wherein said symbols were listed. Furthermore, the directions continue, the creator of the query is commanded to write a portion of it in arabic and some of it in roman and, presumably, God help those who don't know which one when. To further discourage the paying member from cluttering up the newsletter with such dumkopf garbage as queries, there is a final, unchallengeable edict laid out as to who the ABSOLUTE AUTHORITY is in any newsletter decisions regarding anyone having the audacity to approach the editor with a query, ever.

Now, I'll bet you're thinking that all the above roadblocks would just about eliminate queries and query writers altogether, aren't you? Not so. Amazingly, in this recent issue six brave souls actually survived the editorial barrage and were bestowed with space on the query page. I don't know, they must have been Germans and used to those kind of rules. Of course, maybe we'd better not count one of those six, because that particular member was looking for a HOER, and when you are brazen enough to come right out and try to do that sort of thing in print for the whole world to see, it's best not to dignify such a request at all. I don't understand it, the ever-vigilant editor must have been out having a beer and knockwurst when that one slipped past.

What do you do then, you ask, if you've filled in all the latest blanks on your family chart and are facing, eyeball to surname, that obstacle that most of us genealogy hobbyists face sooner or later, a bloody foreigner? Not all of us can cough up the moolah for a research trip overseas. And some of those who could afford it might, under present world tensions, not wish to be taken hostage, blown up, or gunned down while strolling through the burial grounds on foreign soil. Is there a nice, safe alternative? You bet, and it's spelled Salt Lake City.

"Heaven is large, and affords space for all modes of love and fortitude." — Ralph Waldo EMERSON

GAS Attacks
Salt Lake City

First, in case you're puzzling over the above title, I guess it would be in order to give you a little shot of explanation. Just remember, dear reader, that if it ever becomes your sole responsibility, or if you even have a major say in the crucial chore of choosing a moniker for something as important as a genealogical society, for criminy sakes please keep uppermost in your mind just exactly what initials a hastily selected name could saddle you with. Somehow I would guess that the folks up in Sacramento, California never gave the matter a thought, were a tad tipsy on citrus punch the night they picked their name, or, just possibly, were simply being totally and bluntly honest about their condition up there in an area where they grow so much fruit. But the fact is, for the Genealogical Association of Sacramento to be forevermore known as GAS does rather invite titters, if not outright guffaws. Thank God they've got a sense of humor, because I'll bet they come across numerous occasions when they get the chance to exercise it.

77

Whatever it is that propels them, those dedicated GAS-ers do take their genealogy hobby seriously. So fanatical are they that they scrimp and save every spare penny of their housekeeping money with a mad passion so that they can make nearly yearly pilgrimages to that Olympus of dead relative collectors, Salt Lake City. This year, in a light-hearted mood, they invited me to tag along, as a sort of mascot, I guess, little realizing what havoc could result. So it came to pass that around thirty of us zealots, roughly twenty-nine women and one man, pens and notebooks at the ready, briefcases bulging, descended upon Utopia. As luck would have it, it was snowing the day some of us arrived, so we were more than a little grateful to be quartered in a hotel next-door to the building where all the goodies were stored, the LDS Family History Library. Being typical flibbertigibbet Californians, we probably would have froze something up trying to flounder around any further than a half-block in all that white stuff in our sundresses and sandals. (I don't recall the man in our group being so attired—I think he wore a golf cap and sandals, and hopefully something in between.)

Most of us early-birds, who hit town on a Saturday, fully anticipated spending a peaceful evening in quiet meditation, contemplating the particular genealogical projects we planned for Monday, and perhaps watching nothing more than the snowflakes fluttering soundlessly past our hotel windows. After all, we were in Salt Lake City, not exactly known as the fun capital of the world. Little did we know. Unfortunately, the hotel had seen fit to book another gigantic group of boarders earlier that week, a group whose ages appeared to range from about sixteen to nineteen. As you can imagine, they hadn't the slightest intention of spending a quiet Saturday night in the big city, or of letting anyone else spend one either. If you could have somehow pooled their brain-power, I seriously doubt if they could have even collectively come up with the definition of a quiet night. It was not so bad from around 8:00 that evening till about 11:00, when most of their exhuberant activity consisted of running around hysterically in the snowy streets outside. But then they exploded indoors for the night and the din just about done us old-timers in. As near as I could tell, they were conducting various contests in the hallways and in their assorted rooms. One such competition seemed to be a trial to determine who could slam his or her hotel room door shut with the greatest force (this one lasted all through the night). Another amusement involved foot races up and down the hallways, accompanied by screaming. In fact, everything they did was accompanied by screaming. Other sporting events included playing the television at ear-splitting level, phoning every room in the hotel at least a half-dozen times, throwing up rather vocally, knocking heavy objects (persons? furniture?) over in their rooms, and performing God knows what games in the elevators. Where the hotel staff was all night, I can't begin to guess.

Maybe bound and gagged in the office downstairs? Or perhaps after three or four nights of presumably the same type of goings-on they had vacated the premises altogether? Since the energy of these shining examples of the younger generation didn't wane until nearly sun-up, we pooped oldsters emerged in a pretty red-eyed, cranky mood. Oh, by the way, there was one final explosion of noise, a rousing cheer from the hotel maids and us genealogists when the last of the young hooligans checked out. Here's hoping that the whole deafening nightmare was a very rare occurrence, but just in case it wasn't, I'm packing a reliable set of ear-plugs next time I go.

By Sunday morning the rest of our gaggle of GASers, the train-riding bunch, had arrived, revved up and ready. There was not too much to do, however, it being the Sabbath, even for those of us who could manage to keep awake. I went out walking in the snow in a brand-new pair of tennis shoes, which only goes to show you that I wasn't operating on a full complement of cylinders. The blisters that resulted on the heels of my feet were spectacular. The rest of the day we spent nodding and dreaming, thinking of all the major breakthroughs we knew we'd make on the morrow, all the important blanks we'd miraculously be able to fill in on our scanty family charts, thanks to that great library next-door.

The only other activity that there was to participate in was to eat, and if you are a true gourmet, an excellent judge of epicurean delights, you might want to avoid Salt Lake City altogether. I don't know, perhaps the Mormon pioneers were just too busy killing locusts, or erecting statues, or being persecuted to take time out for cooking lessons and to pass the knowledge down to their descendants. Or, more likely, maybe we genealogy hobbyists

simply didn't wander far enough away from the area around the library to discover the really superb four-star eateries that must lurk there somewhere, and if so, I apologize. Actually, in fairness to the eating establishments nearby, they may not try too hard to make a culinary impression on genealogists, and I dare say most of those obsessed creatures (the genealogists) can be recognized immediately by an observant waitress. If it's breakfast time, they don't show up at all for fear of losing a good place in line outside the library. And when they come scurrying in for lunch, sometimes as late as 3:30 so they don't lose their projector, they certainly don't intend to waste their over-strained eyesight reading something as non-genealogical as a menu, so they simply point to the cheapest "special," whatever it is, and scarf it down like they're coming off a twenty-day fast. After all, one can't waste precious mid-day minutes away from the library, can one, not if one expects to make any earth-shattering discoveries, that is. As far as dinner is concerned, just try scaring up a really elegant repast after 10:00 at night (when the library closes on most days). Why, even if you could, you'd probably fall asleep in the vichyssoise after nearly fifteen hours turning the old projector-crank. I'll have to admit, that for a person like me, who might be called a smidgen overweight due to a gluttonous delight in good food, about the only place that I can guarantee to stick to a diet is Salt Lake City, because of the hypnotic pull of the library and the frenzied desire not to miss any time inside.

With all that in mind, that Monday morning I was up like a shot at 5:30 A.M., not wanting to miss out on any of the action. I hadn't ever been to the "new" library, just the old one, and not even there for years, so it would almost be like a maiden voyage. One of the experts with GAS advised me to get out there on the sidewalk and secure a place in line by at least 7:00, and I'd gone so far as to make a test-run on Sunday to determine how many minutes it would take me to limp over there.

Quivering with fired-up enthusiasm, I stood there in my hotel room and went, for the hundredth time that morning, back over my checklist prior to departing for the library, priding myself on being a 100% careful planner who always has everything under complete control. Once again, I bragged to myself, I hadn't overlooked a thing and all details were organized to perfection. I'd thrown a smock over my regular clothes so that I'd have lots of pockets. And the pockets were crammed with everything I'd need: antacids, Anacin, cough drops, Kleenex, pens, paper clips, magnifying glass, nickels and dimes (for the copying machines), and peanuts (which are absolutely forbidden but a good source of protein to keep me from starving to death, if I could get away with it). I'd bring along a jacket, not to wear indoors but to drape over whatever chair I chose in order to send a clear signal to others that it was "taken." In my right hand was clasped a fresh, unspoiled yellow legal tablet, and in my left hand was the thick booklet I'd previously had Xeroxed with all my necessary charts and notes. It was 6:55 A.M.—I was *ready!!!* I took a final big, deep breath of eager anticipation . . . and the zipper on my stretch-Levis broke! So there I was, indecently exposed and caught on the horns of one horrendous dilemma. If I took time to change my pants, I'd be late getting in line, maybe by minutes even. If I just bravely set forth, undone so to speak, I'd have to remember to scrunch over drastically all day long or my severe gaposis would surely be discovered. And, if I sat down anywhere out in the open, what then? Luckily, sanity struck and the change was made. Fortunately, the line was only a half-block long when I hobbled into place.

You realize that when you make such a research trip with a group, you may travel as a group, eat as a group sometimes, and be housed in the same hotel as a group, but when it comes to the library, it's every man for herself. Genealogy is not really a group activity, not unless your whole family gets in it together. I have my ancestors. You have yours. So, as tightly knit a little group as those GAS-ers were, they shot apart like particles of a fireworks burst when that library door opened. Some bolted upstairs, some down, and so the group came ungrouped. I'd studied a map of the place previous to the trip, so as not to get too badly disoriented, and headed, like most of the crowd, upstairs to the United States film floor. Noticing that most

of the scrambling patrons were sprinting for the projectors on the left, I aimed for a row on the right which, for some reason, didn't seem to be attracting as many fans. Once I'd picked what looked like the "best" projector and circled the chair and marked it with my belongings, sort of the same as animals do in the wild, I zipped back to find a microfiche index.

Quickly selecting three numbers from the list I'd made and locating the films that matched the numbers, I raced back to "my" projector. It was at that moment that I discovered the reason I didn't have to indulge in any kind of a fist-fight in order to get a projector in that particular aisle. As a perfect example of my standard run of luck, all the projectors in that row were marked with a taped warning: "USE NARROW FILM *ONLY* ON THIS MACHINE." Guess what my film wasn't? Funny though, looking around at the faster researchers up and down the aisle, who were already busily spinning their cranks, most of them appeared to be in total violation and were viewing *wide* film, warning signs be damned. But, not wanting to get tossed bodily out of the building for gross insubordination, and not by then finding a vacant projector in any other non-restrictive aisle, I retreated downstairs to the book section. That seemed to me to be the wisest move, to bide one's time until someone fainted upstairs and freed a projector.

By the way, I might mention a slight problem the library was experiencing the week we were there, which caused a little more confusion than I would suppose is normal. The powers-that-be had ordered re-carpeting for the entryway, the stairways and heaven knows where else so that you couldn't count on familiar exits and passageways to be where you last left them, at least not so that you could use them at any given time. Sometimes the stairway was closed. Sometimes the area in front of the elevators was closed. One day, first thing in the morning, we found out that the whole blooming lobby was closed and that was the closest I've ever seen a crowd come to rioting. What happened was a young man in a suit came out and announced the predicament to the block-long line and told them that he was going to have to escort them in through the back entrance. Well, some of the younger and more agile persons way back in the line broke ranks and started to sprint for the back of the building. As you can no doubt imagine, this shameful display brought angry screams of protest from those less sprightly who had been standing there since the dawn's early light in the front of the line. The young man in the suit, afraid of getting trampled in the stampede and losing control forever, tried to restore order, but not before a lot of unruly pushing and shoving and near-fisticuffs engulfed the riled up patrons.

The only other time the re-carpeting job could have caused a serious problem, the danger was averted mainly because the people involved were not ordinary human beings but committed research addicts. In that instance, which occurred on a weekday mid-morning, everyone was completely engrossed in his or her own personal microfiche perusing, film viewing or page turning, totally oblivious to everything else. Suddenly a voice came over the loudspeaker announcing that there was a fire in the building and all persons were to leave the building immediately but were not to use the elevators. In any other multi-storied public edifice, with that many occupants, there may have very well been life-threatening pandemonium. In this case, however (at least on the second floor), it was quite the contrary. There was a lot of angry clicking of tongues and I heard more than one voice testily declare, "I'm not going to lose *my* projector, no siree!" And another suspicious soul blurted out, "Do you suppose it's

some kind of a trick to get us away from the projectors?" Finally, when the same voice came on again, urging everyone to follow orders, folks got up from their chairs, reluctantly, and grudgingly plodded off in the direction of the stairs. But, lo and behold, the stairs were blocked off! And we had been warned not to take the elevators. So there we stood, stationary. About that time I had the distinct feeling that a number of the patrons were going to bolt, not for any possible windows or anything like that, but straight back to their projectors. Luckily, and with not a minute to spare, the voice interrupted our mutinous thoughts, saying the fire had been put out. With that, everyone happily about-faced.

One of the things that really puzzled me about the LDS Family History Library, I don't mind admitting, was its deserted rest rooms. I can't speak first-hand about the men's facilities, not being that liberated, but I swear that I never saw another human being in the women's comfort stations. Come to think of it, I rarely saw anyone using the drinking fountains either, which could have a direct tie-in, I suppose. It wouldn't take an EINSTEIN, of course, to deduce that the main reason for this phenomenon was that one didn't come all the way to Salt Lake City just to urinate, by golly! Not by a long shot! That would be taking valuable time away from research. So, if you notice a little more squirming going on down your aisle mid-morning or mid-afternoon, don't be surprised.

The other thing that becomes rather obvious, after spending some time in the library, is that not too many people get too worked up about the various signs posted hither and yon. Just as the sign mentioned above, instructing patrons to use only a certain type of film in certain projectors, didn't generate much compliance, other signs are ignored as well. Maybe, you say, I'm a fine one to be casting stones, running around with peanuts (and sometimes candy bars) in my pocket, when I knew full well that eating was verboten in the research areas of the library. But I wasn't the only one. There seemed to be violators all over the place. For instance, there was a reasonable rule about the number of films anyone should take at any one time. Even I was willing to abide by that one, since I hadn't yet figured out a way of viewing more than one film at a time. Yet some individuals had a pile of reels resembling the Empire State Building nestled securely at their work stations. Another notice that didn't command much respect was the one saying that if you were planning to be away from your projector for more than a certain period of time, you should give it up. Why, some of the projectors in my immediate vicinity sat idle (but draped with their user's belongings) for long enough that the user could have darned near made a round-trip to Provo in the meantime. Understandably though, most of us would have rather parted with a loved one than with "our" projector, so the library administration may have to concede that directive. Surprisingly, most genealogists complied pretty well with the sign on my favorite copying machine, asking users to limit themselves to five copies at a turn, then take a place at the end of the line, thereby giving the next person in line a shot. Maybe that was because I, almost coming unglued at spotting the long lines at copying machines on the floor I was on, sought out and found, by some miracle, a machine that was a little more hidden and not as popular as most (and if you think I'm going to let you in on the secret of its location, you're crazy). Besides, there is the distinct possibility that it was in somebody's private office, I think.

I noticed a marked contrast between the United States

floor and the European floor. Everything was much more subdued and orderly on the European floor. Not much sign of frivolity anywhere. And there were unoccupied projectors all over the place the week that we were there. It's probably just as well because, if the Hungarian films I had managed to sit through are any indication, a person needs all the power he or she can muster to be able to concentrate for very long on all that foreign stuff. Don't get me wrong, it wasn't completely quiet in there by any means. There was this continuous chatter, very little of which was in English, back and forth between the various projector operators (it was almost like being back home in California, come to think of it). No one tried to initiate a conversation with me. Since I only had complete mastery over *oui, nyet,* and *un burro is muy simpatico,* it's probably just as well.

The European book stacks on that floor were equally puzzling, it seemed to me. For starters, most of the blooming books weren't even in English, giving a patron like me a doozy of a time figuring out where one country's books started and another country's books stopped. But amazingly, other folks were standing around in the book aisles and actually reading the things! So I decided to try to act blasé too, said "Hmmm, how interesting" a lot, pulled various volumes down from here and there and tried to figure out if I had each one right-side-up. I'm sure there might be some of you who would be so bold as to suggest that a person with my limited linguistic capabilities was jolly well wasting her time in the European book section. What in the world, you might ask, was I doing there? That's a stupid question. Trying to find books that might be Hungarian, French, Czechoslovakian, German and Polish is what I was doing. Why ever for, you ask? Well, the copying machine ain't choosy. It will even copy those

alien kind of books and if I could recognize any words that looked even vaguely helpful, I planned to go ahead and feed in my nickels and give the machine a workout. So what if I didn't understand zip of what I copied. Hope springs eternal and there was always the possibility that someday I'd find someone who did. Isn't that what foreign research is all about?

Before I exit the European floor, I'd just like to say that you'll find the nicest, most patient volunteers helping patrons on that floor, especially the young people who are doing so. How they can keep their cool and go on smiling and being courteous in the face of such stupidity should earn them gold medals of some sort. For instance, whenever I got impatient with the copying machine on that floor and pressed the wrong buttons, and it jammed, the young man would just smile and fix it, talking calmly all the while like one would do to patients in a nursing home.

And when I'd make a request for six Hungarian films to be brought up from the vaults at 8:30 at night, the young woman would just smile, fill in the official forms and go fetch them. So, to those volunteers, and to others all over that fantastic library—a *big* "THANK YOU."

One event the officers with GAS had promised, back when they were first touting their group trip for the year, failed to materialize, through no fault of GAS. Actually, we all gained more from the spontaneously substituted activity, when you get right down to it. The organization had booked a local expert to give a presentation to and answer questions from our group on a Monday night (a night the library closes earlier than 10:00). They'd scheduled him well in advance, sent his fee, got confirmation, and booked a room large enough to hold all of us. But, as it turned out, the speaker never did arrive. Nor did he, or anyone else, communicate an excuse. So there we sat, fidgeting around in our folding chairs, looking expectantly at poor Donna VAN LONE, the group leader, as if she could miraculously wave a magic wand and pull the !@#$%¢&*() speaker out of a hat somehow. If I were Donna about that time, I would have bloody well panicked, run sobbing from the assemblage and barricaded myself in my hotel room in a blue funk. But not Donna. She stood up there with a brave smile on her face and gave us the whole sorry story. Then she suggested, since we had paid for the room and were all together, that we just improvise our own danged program by having each one there confide to the audience her, or his, aspirations in genealogy for this particular trip and any significant discoveries already made that first day. Ho hum, I thought, we'll be here all night. But it turned out to be pretty interesting because there were some doggoned knowledgeable GASers present who could have given "how-to" speeches in their own right and been a blasted sight more informative than some I've heard. For instance, one person would mention a very rare surname they were seeking and the state in which they were hoping to find same, and someone else in the room would pop up with the suggestion that they try such-and-such a county because they'd run across a whole passel of that surname there while hunting for their own. Another individual would complain about a particular county and its lack of cooperation, and darned if there wasn't a person in the audience who had worked with a much more helpful source in the same county and was willing to share the necessary name and address. In some cases, I couldn't believe my ears. It was a fantastic evening, as it turned out, because here were plain everyday hobbyists helping each other. And most of us were taking notes just as frantically as if we were being indoctrinated by a real live speaker. You've got to hand it to those Sacramentoites, if they've got nothing better up there at all, they've got GAS.

Realistically speaking, I'm not certain that everyone in our hobby of genealogy has the time, money, or even good enough health to be able to make a trip to that Elysium of hunting grounds that is Salt Lake City. Regardless, except for the seriously homebound, most of us can accomplish at least a portion of our research through our post office box. You can certainly learn more about that citadel of confusion, the military, in this manner, probably even enough to turn you into an instant conscientious objector. Please plow on . . .

"Men love war because it allows them to look serious. Because it is the one thing that stops women laughing at them." — John FOWLES

Duck!
It's a Minié Ball!

One thing you can count on when fiddling around with the military, is that you never know what surprises will ambush you along the way. But I'm getting a tad ahead of the regiment here. Before we march our forces forth on this subject, we'd best call a halt until we can fire off to you bewildered beginners some elementary marching orders. Attention! First, don't suppose for a moment that you will be able to get your grubby hands on old military, pension and bounty-land records by just writing a neat, personal letter for them. You couldn't possibly think it would be that easy. You should know your government better than that by now. Ever since we skewered our last invading Redcoat with a trusty bayonet, our government has been engaging in the cursed practice of transforming every simple procedure into something hopelessly complicated. Perhaps they figure that's the only security they have for staying in office. It would take too many incomprehensible official forms, with all the blanks filled in, to

GENERIC REQUEST FORMS | TRIPLICATE FORMS | DUPLICATE FORMS | FORMS TO TRACK MISSING REQUESTS | FORMS FOR CHECKING REQUEST FORMS | REQUESTS FOR LISTS OF REQUEST FORMS

I AM FROM THE GOVERNMENT AND I AM HERE TO HELP YOU

throw the schemers out. Accordingly, they will only accept hand-writ letters from you if they are requests for government forms. Otherwise you must use an approved official form to communicate with them. But they are reasonably big-hearted about doling out forms. "What the heck!" they say, with a devil-may-care attitude. And, so long as you and other taxpayers keep footing the bill every April 15th, they'll probably go on being magnanimously compliant. However, they do reserve the right to call the shots by disputing the number of forms you may so greedily request, and then arbitrarily sending you whatever amount they decide is best. The government always knows better than you do about what's good for you. Additionally, you are admonished, you must list whatever form you are attempting to pry out of them by its official government printing office number, or they won't play. So ask for NATF Form 80 (unless they've changed it by now).

Each NATF Form 80 contains four pages, three in duplicate, wouldn't you know. One would think, unless the filler-inner was more than a little mentally deficient, that the federals wouldn't have to use the entire remaining fourth page for directions on how to fill in the form, but that's the way it is. Among other crystal-clear instructions, it says not to use this form for wars from World War One forward and to use a separate form each for the military records (which it pompously claims genealogists couldn't possibly give a tinker's doggone about anyway) as opposed to pension records, except for those connected to the Revolutionary War, in which case you just use one for both, but don't put both of anything in any one envelope because they CAN ONLY HANDLE ONE AT A TIME, for Pete's sake, and make sure you enclose all three color-coded duplicate pages, which had better be in their virgin state and not ripped apart, and furthermore you shouldn't even contemplate trying to pull a fast one like counterfeiting these official forms by photocopying them because they have G-men back there armed with German Shepherds ready to leave at a moment's notice and head your way.

Eureka, I'll be hornswoggled!!! Guess what I just this minute found? Not only is the instruction page covered all over one side with directions, but the blithering drivel is all over the back side too. (I guess the reason I never noticed it for all these years is that I have a particular loathing for instruction sheets of any kind and simply tear them up and throw them away.) Well, I guess a person is never too much of an expert to learn something new. No, on second thought, after carefully scrutinizing what I'd been missing for so long, I don't think it would have smartened me up one iota if I had found it any earlier.

The actual NATF Form 80 itself, in triplicate, is rela-

tively uncomplicated. (Maybe I shouldn't make this statement because the government might get wind of it and
realize they'd slipped up badly and revise it, heaven forbid.) The way it is now, even a beginner might be in
danger of being able to figure out how to fill in the blanks.
Then, once it's on its snail-pace way to Washington, D.C.,
don't expect to hear anything back from it the same year
you send it in, necessarily, not unless it's early in the year.
They're stacked up to their armpits back there all the time,
or so they would laughingly have us believe, so it's best
not to get antsy. When the return envelope does put in an
appearance, the first round of suspense is over, once
you've opened it to discover whether the National
Archives staff has decided to honor you by hunting for
and finding something. If you won the toss of their coin
and they announce that they do have some records for
you, you will gratefully write a check for $5.00 and, along
with the infernal proper form, get it off in the earliest mail.
And wait some more. Someday, however, all your suspense will be over when your mailman, or mailwoman,
hands over that large yellow packet.

Now I, for one, will openly disagree with the federalee who composed the instructional page, both sides of it, on the above form. The anonymous writer, probably in a deliberate attempt to push for more federal holidays and shorter working hours, tries to discourage genealogists from sending for the military records at all, saying they aren't very "useful." Useful they may not be, but fascinating they very often are, at least most of them that I've seen. For instance, the Civil War ones generally tell you the hair and eye color of your long ago recruit, whether he'd been out in the sun too long, how tall he stood, where he'd been born and what he swore was his age (not always true), and what he might have listed as his civilian job. Then, depending on what happened to the fellow after he was mustered in, the military records could also contain prisoner-of-war information, charges that he'd decided to take French leave, names of some of the locations he'd involuntarily found himself in, amounts he may have been fined for losing something important, like his musket, sick leave and sometimes court martial reports, just all sorts of colorful little tidbits. And you'll only have to shell out $5.00. So go ahead, pay no attention to what they say.

As an example, one early member of our family, who happens to be a direct ancestor of the only living celebrity we've found in our family to date, managed to survive the whole Civil War in the army, enlisting twice. So his military file has a number of interesting items. He had to "forfeit one mos. pay proper" by sentence of a regimental court martial, in the first month of his service, no less, but whatever he did must not have been too serious and wasn't explained. He'd lost his "Ordnance" (gun) three times and got fined $15.46 each time. Since his pay was listed as $13.00 a month, for awhile he wound up paying the government in order to go on fighting for it. Uncle

Sam also handed him a bill for $22.72 "for transporta-
tion." In those days, it seems, you sometimes had to give
more than your blood for your country.

Another military file in my possession details excitement of another sort—however confusing—concerning
yet another early relative. It states that he was captured in
Lafayette, Georgia, perished as a prisoner-of-war on the
steamer *Sultana* when she blew up on the Mississippi
River about a week after the war had ended, and still
managed to apply for a pension, lose his hand while building a bridge in 1872 and die (again?) in 1912. (???)

As in every war, lots of the boys lied about their age
and, if you check carefully, you might catch them at it.
One sad case I found, a brother of the first one above, had
apparently, with his brother's help, claimed to be nineteen

when, in fact, he was barely seventeen. He joined his brother's unit. Both fought at the Battle of Cloyd's Mountain, Virginia, but the youngster was wounded and taken prisoner. Incarcerated in Emory & Henry College, which was doing duty as a makeshift hospital, the boy died a month later of his wounds, surrounded by his enemies. He wasn't allowed to be buried in the fenced-in part of the nearby cemetery in holy ground, being a "damn Yankee," but after the war he was taken by wagon to the cemetery in Nashville, folks there being a bit more tolerant. All because he lied about his age.

One person who also prevaricated, but in the other direction, may have been trying to escape one of his five wives. An uncle of the two brothers above, he swore to being "forty-fore" years old, when the family Bible and his first marriage license application prove he was actually forty-nine. He lasted nearly a year at that, until the company doctor declared the poor wretch was "50 years old and much broken down" and sent him back to the missus. He couldn't have been *too* broken down, leastways not all parts of him, because he married two more women and sired three more kids after the war.

Of course the pension rolls should cough up more of your needed genealogical information, especially if the veteran (or widow) involved had the tenacity to hang in there, determined to get the blasted pension. They had to deal with government regulations in those days, too, and come up with a ridiculous number of certified, notarized, recorded forms, declarations and affidavits. I'm sure some of the statements in the affidavits were a tad exaggerated. I've even found one that was, in all fairness, disallowed for a fairly good reason. It seems that two ladies in different parts of Indiana both applied for a pension under the same veteran. They may have, truthfully, both been under the same veteran at some time, but the government didn't want to hear about it, not when he was finally resting peacefully and nothing could be proved.

In another interesting case, the father of the seventeen-year-old, above, hoping to go on being a man of leisure, applied for a Father's Pension after his young son was killed. At the beginning of the war he (the father) had chosen a second wife from a prosperous family loaded with judges, doctors and money, probably figuring that should take care of his needs. In fairness to his new in-laws, they were doing their utmost to subsidize the bounder in the manner to which he'd become accustomed. Further trying to be accommodating, they each went out on a limb for him after the war by filing affidavits stating that he was at death's door and needed immediate help. (These were submitted before his last four children were born, so you be the judge.) There's even a postscript to this case. A few years ago I met a descendant from the same prosperous family which had had the bad fortune to hook up with ours and be saddled with the care of my free-loading relative. Don't let anyone tell you that history doesn't repeat itself. She invited me to stay at her house in Ohio, showing that she'd inherited the best of her family's traditions. And I accepted, proving that I'd inherited the worst of mine.

Regulations were just as cumbersome for the Revolutionary War veterans and their widows. One of my PARENT line has a pension file so thick it darn near needs its own separate file cabinet. His problem seemed to be that, by the time he got around to applying for a pension, so many of his comrades-in-arms had Gone to Their Reward that there weren't many left to amble on down to the courthouse to fill in the necessary documents for him. Another fly in the ointment was that he couldn't seem to remember whether he'd been a private or a sergeant, which made a difference, I understand, in terms of the largesse grudgingly doled out. He did manage to round up one old duffer and get him to come in and sign a statement. The old guy said (and probably somewhat angrily) that he sure would swear my kin was in the army because the rascal had come out to their house with his platoon in the middle of the war and arrested his brother for draft dodging.

Part of the confusion in that war was the result of the rather loosely interpreted terms of enlistment. No one knew which soldier had crops to tend at home, so how was anyone to know when any individual man would decide to take an unauthorized furlough in order to go home and harvest? After two full years of filling in forms and badgering others to do so on his behalf, my relative did what we'd probably do today, bribe a congressman to go to bat for him. He immediately got his pension. Four months later he was back in the courthouse to fill in another form, this time to confess that after he'd received his long-awaited pension certificate, he'd lost it while riding a horse between Trenton and Freehold.

Some pension files will set you to singing. Others may cause blue smoke to rise. The great ones are those that contain marriage licenses, Bible records, and spouse's and offspring's names, among other treasures. The maddening ones are those that mention wife and children but never divulge their names. But worse than that are the consarned ancestors who were too filthy rich or too aggravatingly proud to apply for a pension at all. So you take your chances but it's usually well worth it.

Now, a word to you old timers in the hobby. When you first started to dig up dead relatives, you may have been doing it as a lark, or because your best friend was hooked. Then it became a challenge. Later you became hopelessly addicted. But now that you have thirty-two file cabinets full of records, fifteen briefcases full of certificates, and very little energy left, what is to become of all of it? If you follow modern trends, no one attempts to do the slightest thing nowadays without "Formulating a Plan" and "Setting a Goal." It's the "in" thing to do. The first move you'll want to remember is to turn the page.

"In creating, the only hard thing's to begin; / A grass blade's no easier to make than an oak." — James Russell LOWELL

How to Make Sure Your Goal is Showing

Have you ever, especially when the main thrust of your genealogical research has ground to a screeching halt, sat down quietly and pondered where in the world you were headed with your glorious hobby? The first piece of advice any professional know-it-all always seems to stick in advice books is that tired old admonition to "Set a Goal," which they invariably try to jam down the reader's throat. So it behooves me to follow suit. Now I'm not quite so stupid as to try to direct this message toward those *very* sanctimonious hobbyists, quite often missing altogether any kind of a recognizable sense of humor, who are convinced that genealogy is some kind of a super pious pilgrimage, never to be touched with anything but evangelical solemnity. Their motivation is far too right-eous to mess with. Besides, they wouldn't touch any advice offered by an upstart like me with a ten-foot pole. Freely acknowledging this state of affairs, I'm taking aim at the rest of you, those who accidentally fell into the hobby and found it to be fun, those who thought it might be a jim-dandy way to keep the old brain cells slogging along, and even those of you who fiendishly enjoy snooping around, digging up the family dirt. You're the ones who are in grave need of a goal.

Now, to get you to stop nodding off and start paying attention, please try to put yourself in the following scenario. Suppose one of those flying saucers from outer space (you know, the kind they're always seeing in Mississippi and places like that where there's not much else to attract their attention) swooped down and landed smack dab in the middle of your front lawn and the little green aliens aboard decided to take you back with them as their captive, and no one on earth ever saw you again . . . just what do you suppose would happen to all that hard work of yours? Would your file cabinets be on the next garbage truck out of town? Think about it.

To illustrate this point, I had a female first-cousin who had two favorite hobbies, men and genealogy. In between five husbands of her own, and no telling how many belonging to others, she spent a fortune hiring professional genealogists to look up and send her information on our family history. Rumor had it that they came up with all sorts of startling new revelations about our ancestors. Her sister even claimed she'd made a surprise discovery wherein our mysterious French ancestor turned out to be an Italian. Then, before she could share all her treasures with the rest of the family, she up and died. Now none of her husbands, or anyone else for that matter, can find her voluminous files. So all her efforts and tremendous expense went for nothing.

Many of you have already found the solution to this exasperating problem. It's a simple one. Share what you

have with others *now*. Don't wait for that rosy day that's always lurking somewhere in the future, that day you keep assuring yourself that you are going to, quote, "write that book," unquote. "One of these days" just never comes. *That day is now!* You don't even have to fork over a lot of money to do a formally published book. If you share with just one other person, you immediately double the odds of having your hard work survive for the future.

As an example, let me tell you about a neat lady back in Illinois with whom I correspond. A couple of years ago she had passed her eightieth birthday and was beginning to experience seriously failing eyesight. She'd been infected with genealogy many years previously and said she had always hoped to write a book but now she knew she never would. She didn't think any of her close kin were particularly interested in the family history, although she allowed as how they might be someday. I kept nagging her and nagging her, by letter, to try to do something about writing it down. Finally, partly in self-defense, I suppose, to get me off her back, she began writing in her beautiful Palmer Method longhand (in the kind of a lined tablet that school children use) all her priceless recollections about her family branch, black sheep and white, and its stories and charts. When she'd finished the entire tablet, she sent it to me to keep. That tablet became one of my most precious research tools, but that wasn't the end of the story. That dear lady, who had somehow managed, even under such difficult circumstances, to conquer that little lined tablet, got so charged up doing so that she went triumphantly ahead and accomplished what she had always dreamed she would. Her published hardback book came out last summer.

I've stopped horsing around long enough to tell you the above story for just one reason—to goose you into some action of your own.

Earlier this year one of the nearby genealogical societies to which I belong decided that the time was right to attempt to goad its membership into making some kind of a try at preserving its records. Accordingly, they scheduled what they hoped would turn into a regular monthly workshop for authors and would-be authors. I figured I certainly should go to that one because I'd been so busy the last few years writing books that I hadn't been able to spare the time to go to any kind of counseling session telling me how to do it, and, Lord knows, I sure could use the help (as I've no doubt you have perceived by now and would heartily agree).

About twenty-five to thirty eager souls drifted in to that first get-together, all motivated to the hilt, I presumed. The fellow who had thought up the brainstorm for having such a meeting in the first place quickly pounced on the gavel and announced that he would be the chairman. Then, perhaps thinking he had to justify such a presumptuous takeover, he proceeded to fill us in laboriously on his qualifications. This step probably wasn't really necessary since no one else had dreams of power fanatical enough to challenge him or try to arm-wrestle him for the podium. He did admit that he had not actually written anything himself as yet, but that he was "hoping to someday" and that he had gone to a "how-to" meeting once and took notes. Then he wandered a bit off the path by letting us all in on the myriad details of his own personal research (much the same as I keep doing in this book, come to think of it). But he was a lot more thorough, supplying us with all the intricate facts that he had obtained from scores of relatives he had contacted, accompanied by a minute history of the main surname he was researching. Before long, folks began to fidget. One of the more antsy gentlemen, undoubtedly expecting something a shade different on the program, broke into the droning monologue with the suggestion that the chairman ask each person in the room to introduce himself or herself and to confess their goals. The chairman, trying to personify democracy in action, grudgingly acquiesced.

One person said she represented a local printing shop, and may have been hunting for business. Another was a computer fanatic (I warned you that they are everywhere) and if the subject wasn't about computers, he didn't want to talk about it. Three of us were authors, if you could seriously call us that, and the remainder were in every stage imaginable, all the way from being just weeks into the hobby to having a 5,000-page manuscript (of sorts) "almost ready." No one there at that first meeting could even vaguely be considered an expert. Especially me, since my then current book, *Collecting Dead Relatives,* had been officially ignored by the officers of that particular genealogical society because of an accusation that I had poked fun at one of their meetings (as if I'd ever stoop so low as to do such a thing).

So, once we got done with the round-robin show-and-tell, there was not much left to do except argue about what the best date would be to have the next meeting. Once that monumental decision had been reached, the folks who hadn't yet left the meeting out of boredom were free to jump into a debate on selecting the specific phase of genealogy book-writing to pursue at the next meeting. No one there proposed another stimulating recitation by the chairman, perhaps to his chagrin, but he wasn't going to give up on the one topic which, he admitted, caused a burning sensation in his breast—"The Numbering System." And so, in order to be allowed to adjourn for the day, we agreed to his topic.

In breathless anticipation the days flew past, and before I had scarcely recovered from the first one, the second meeting was upon us. This time only about nine people could tear themselves free to attend (I suspect the rest were home writing their books, unaided). The chairman, quivering happily with the thought of launching us into the electrifying subject of numbering systems, started off the discussion by graciously giving us his formula for instant success in the matter. He charged that for much too long a time spouses of ancestors in family histories had been treated like dirt and he intended liberating his by giving them all their very own separate numbers. That pronouncement caused a couple of women, who had up until that point been peacefully sitting there exchanging knitting patterns, to leap aggressively into the fray and tell the chairman his idea stunk. Before they could come to blows, a previously silent gentleman announced simply, "I'm not going to use any numbers at all." Obviously, not too many converts were swayed by this radical declaration, and the knitters even went so far as to move to the other side of the table, perhaps hoping the latest idea wasn't contagious.

Well, the meeting about numbering systems labored on for an hour or so and it became obvious that each individual there was going to cling to his or her own chosen system as the absolute cat's pajamas. No sir, no one was about to exchange theirs for any of the other lame-brained suggestions, not on a bet. In the waning moments of that thrill-packed morning, the chairman wistfully closed the door on his favorite subject, promising everyone that they would return to it next time. Then, as an afterthought, he asked if there were any other questions. One fellow, almost surrounded by briefcases, piped up, "How can we try to make family histories less boring?" (Pretty good question, I thought.) He was nearly ready to go to his publisher, he said, holding up a massive typed manuscript to prove it, "And I can't even get my wife to read this!"

I hung in there, gentle reader, through one more entire meeting, where only three potential writers showed up, the word having gotten around, I suppose. Then I called it quits. It seems to me that, if your goal is to write a book, it might make more sense to just stay home, drag out the old typewriter, and do it. It isn't going to do itself while you're off someplace getting yourself all befuddled in "how-to" sessions.

So, if you're sitting there today, pregnant with your own book and about to give birth someday soon, what can you expect from other people? A growing sense of indifference? Maybe. Opposition to it altogether from other members of your family (especially when you hit them with the horrendous fee it's going to take to do it)? That too maybe. You see, no matter how revved up you may be over the possibility of seeing your work in print, others may remain a little limp. But when it comes right down to it, it only takes one person to know that you can do it, and that's *you*. So stick to it, regardless.

The biggest problem I had getting *Collecting Dead Relatives* ready to be published was finding an illustrator. It isn't the type of item housewives are expected to go out everyday and locate by instinct. And contrary to what some folks may have guessed, Randy CALHOUN, the illustrator for that book and this one, is not my little nephew or some other kind of relative. CALHOUN

sounds too much like a blasted Confederate to have dared come within shooting distance of my staunch Unionist kinfolk, much less married into our family. Just what was a person supposed to do, I wondered, when suddenly faced with the necessity of rounding up someone who could draw more than stick figures or dirty pictures? Well, as you might imagine, the first place I turned to was my own family. Our oldest daughter is an artist in her own right, but at that particular time in her life she was too busy trying to get pregnant to stay upright long enough to draw pictures. And then I had a niece over in the desert of Nevada who had become a well-known western artist, but unless I wanted the book filled up with sketches of Herefords and sagebrush, she didn't seem like a good choice either. Meanwhile, the months slipped by, leaving me eyeball to eyeball with a quandary.

I had no drawings, no idea of where to find anyone to do any, and had almost decided to do them myself, which would have been a total disaster. It was summertime by then, so I couldn't even go to the local colleges in hopes of luring a starving art student. About that time I had an appointment for the usual three-month resurrection at my hairdresser's and I slunk into the beauty salon, thoroughly depressed. When I started griping about the problem to my hairdresser, she said she just happened to have a friend who just happened to be an illustrator and she gave me his phone number. I called him up that very evening and invited him to come up to my house and show me his etchings. He fell for that old line and it worked out fine. Just goes to show you, if you ever have a problem that needs solving, ask your hairdresser. They can scrounge around and come up with anything! (And I sure hope Randy can't read because if he gets a load of this paragraph he may quit.)

Now, back to the other stumbling blocks you can expect to contend with in your own book-writing adventure . . . Once you have passed the point of staggering through the nightmare of coming up with the magic number of copies to order, you will then be poised on the threshold of that period known as "panic time." That officially begins when a monster truck pulls into your driveway and the driver off-loads enough boxes of books to form something the size of Mt. Everest right there in your very own living room, more books than you've ever seen in your whole life, short of in a bookstore. That's the time to gulp nervously, sit down fast, take an antacid (or a good stiff shot), and wonder if anyone other than your mother will ever buy a copy. If you really get panicked, like I was, because you think you've jumped in way over your head, you send out a little flier to everyone in the United States of America that you can find a name and address for and an indication that they are into genealogy.

However, with the constantly escalating cost of postage stamps, even metered ones, you might find this type of mass advertising is tantamount to subsidizing the U.S. Postal Service. Therefore, you may prefer to take a chance with a book review. But to get a book review, you generally have to send a book, a complimentary one. (Complimentary is a polite term for free.) Then you pray that the book reviewer can read, comprehend, and didn't have a fight with his or her spouse that day. An excellent example of a book review of *Collecting Dead Relatives* came from Mary SIMS with GAS (Genealogical Association of Sacramento). So what success I've had, I can say I owe partly to GAS. Mary said, for some peculiar reason, that she took the book to the bathroom with her. Folks who had long been used to Montgomery Wards catalogs assumed that Mary had discovered a modern alternative and orders poured in, sometimes as many as two and three a day, from people who wanted to give it a try.

But the most prestigious, high-brow review to date on that particular book appeared in a very formal publication out of Nova Scotia. The reader can tell right away that *The Nova Scotia Genealogist* has class because it's typeset on a good grade paper and even has French words in it and a president named Terrence M. PUNCH with a lot of ABCs after his name. Somehow one has the feeling that Terrence M. PUNCH doesn't do his reading in the bathroom. Well, Terrence himself wrote the review and I'll quote the first sentence: "It is a while since I read a genealogical book while doubled up in laughter, of the sort the author intended, at any rate." He also used the word cathartic and some other big words I can't pronounce, so I think it's probably favorable.

But before you let any of the semi-complimentary reviews go to your head and cause you to rush out and buy a bigger hat size, you had better gird yourself for that unpleasant bombshell, the inevitable negative review. My first one on that particular book came from Minnesota, in the dead of winter, so maybe that was partly the reason. They don't appreciate anyone trying to get cutesy with them while their teeth are chattering in all that snow, I guess. The reviewer, displaying enough umbrage to sink the *Lusitania* all over again, said she didn't think the book was the least bit funny, but that it certainly more than lived up to its promise of being irreverent, harumph! Well, you can bet that vitriolic tongue-lashing took the helium out of my balloon.

I had been a mite prepared for the negative side of things, however, because I'd already received one of those slaps in the kisser from the local society I told you about,

when they finally got around to acknowledging the gift of a copy of my family history a year-and-a-half after I donated it to them. The reviewer, a male this time (I'm not bigoted, I alienate at random), charged (and rightly so) that my family history lacked a formal bibliography, which, he said, should be mandatory in genealogies. One of these days I'm anxious to arrange a meeting with the guy to ask him how he would go about preparing a bibliography for a text composed of court records and census listings, a feat I must have missed learning about in school. He also said I should have explained the numbering system (maybe it's the air in this valley that causes so many folks to get freaked-out about numbering systems?) in more complete detail in a separate introduction to the family charts. Funny, I've always thought that two coming after one, and three following two, was pretty basic and that most of us who had managed to get beyond grammar school could handle such simple progression without being thrown into a state of blind panic, but perhaps such is not the case and I'd better watch my numbering from here on in. I wonder if he could have been reading the thing backwards?

So much for depressing subjects . . .

Now, not all of you may feel sadistic enough to turn a book loose on the general public. You may have spent your whole life, up till now, avoiding even writing letters. And here I am, trying to cram a gigantic indigestible writing pill down your gullet. Well, you don't have to sit there and swallow it. If you have a needle handy (preferably not the kind you stick in your arm), you can take aim at a different goal altogether.

"Accidents will happen in the best-regulated families."
— Charles DICKENS

Sew Those So-and-Sos Into a Quilt

"QUILTS???" you ask yourself, "Why is this crazy old broad bringing up such a subject in a genealogy-related book, anyway?" Well, the explanation is really quite simple. Quilts relate to beds, right? Beds were usually the first, and in some cases the only, pieces of furniture your ancestors built, borrowed, begged or stole. Now, put beds and ancestors together and what do you get? Descendants! Genealogy, *voilà!*

It has been a surprise to me to have found so many genealogy hobbyists also into quilt-making. (I may have lost the men here, but they can just jump over to the next chapter.) I can't imagine whoever's left using any of their precious time to digress from research long enough to sit by the hour and cut up material into little pieces and then sew them back together again, but maybe that's what a person progresses to (or backward from?) after very many years in genealogy. And it can't be that only my few acquaintances have gone that way, because genealogical seminars and conferences seem to be offering the subject of quilting quite frequently these days. Actually, it doesn't require an overabundance of intelligence to be able to thread a needle and jam it into a piece of cloth, just reasonable eyesight, I guess, so even a man ought to be able to master it.

The LDS store in Salt Lake City had some absolutely gorgeous handmade quilts on display the last time I was there, the type you could buy and proudly hand down to grandchildren (and lie to them that you'd sewn it by the light of a kerosene lantern in between killing Indians from the driver's seat of your covered wagon—that being the time period most grandchildren think we grandparents date back to anyway). Or, if you're not afraid to tackle such an undertaking yourself, you could do that type of quilt on your own, perhaps following an old-fashioned pattern handed down in your family.

But I have a suggestion for a different theme, one that would truly tie your own family to the final result. Why don't you try to design each square to represent something which has happened in your family or something unique to its members? Before I got hooked on genealogy I started one of these (and, if the truth be known, may never get it finished). Each corner square is the traced hand of one of each of our four children, forever captured in appliqué, identified with the name and birthdate of each. Not terribly imaginative, I realize, but those are the conservative squares. I've let the devil take the hindmost on the rest of them. One is a back view of our old Volkswagen bug with the mutt that was then our family pet sticking its mangy head out the window. Another is a stirring rendition of an old authentic wooden outhouse we borrowed from an uncle when our plumbing went on the blink. Yet another square will forevermore remind us of the fourteen-inch thick, steel-reinforced concrete bomb shelter we constructed ourselves as a family project when the Russkies started messing around down in Cuba (and stocked with cases of wine and imported cheese and volumes of Shakespeare, just in case). So you see, the possibilities are endless. You could do scenes from your own life or, if you've never done much of anything, from the lives of your ancestors.

You could depict a rough version of a gallows, if one of your forebears went that way, or a brilliant scarlet letter "A", à la HAWTHORNE, if that were the appropriate direction. You might even give some thought to the commercial possibilities of letting your quilt help finance some of your genealogical projects. An instant sale would be guaranteed, for instance, were you to create squares listing the correct birthdates of all the living female members of your family (as opposed to the later dates they may be falsely claiming today). Whatever you do, design your quilt to reflect your family's individuality. One genealogist I know, were she to take my advice, could turn out a weird design indeed. Her surname is HOGGETT and she told me her early family members must have had a pork fixation, or a mighty peculiar sense of humor, since they deliberately went out and sought marriage partners named PIGGETT, BACON and HAM.

Some of you may be holding back a bit on the designing aspect of quilting. Don't let the fact that art was the one subject you faithfully dodged in school throw you for a loss. You can always call yourself a primate, like me. (Funny, I thought the word was primitive, but Randy CALHOUN, who has seen my work, says that this is the word that best describes what it looks like did it.) So if I can do it, you can too. Go ahead, let your imagination run rampant.

No matter how wild and colorful you make your family quilt, I doubt that it could ever match in excitement a certain spectacle I'd like to share with you, the memories of which are indelibly etched on my mind in technicolor, wide-screen and 3-D. Please read on . . .

> *"My experience with public libraries is that the first volume of the book I inquire for is out, unless I happen to want the second, when that is out."* — Oliver Wendell HOLMES

Librarians Runnin' Wild

If you ever get yourself identified as an "author," no matter how loosely, you can just naturally expect to receive important invitations to speak in famous, exotic places. Amazingly, that even holds true for genealogy books. Shortly after my little paperback came out, I *knew* I'd hit the big time when I got a formal request to go to Stockton, California in mid-January, in the eye of a major wind-storm. *That's* recognition, by golly! The invitation read, in part, "We never have a regular speaker in January. Our membership doesn't expect much at that meeting because that's when we have all our annual reports and our installation of officers, so not too many people show up." Not exactly overwhelming enthusiasm, it would appear to me, but probably on a par with my oratorical ability, so it couldn't hurt. Who knows? Today Stockton—tomorrow the world! And I might have even done better down there had I not had laryngitis and my arm in a sling due to a broken wrist from falling over my dog. But that's another story.

At least none of the fifty or so folks who had bravely ventured out in that tornado had fallen asleep, even though my part didn't come until the end of a very long program and the room was, as they always are, over-heated. Now, I don't take credit for drawing such a crowd because, as it turned out, I believe each one of them there was on the agenda in one form or another, either to give a report, to be sworn in, or to be singled out for bringing cookies, or for performing something else vital. They were pretty fascinating reports, most of them, except for the auditor's. That poor lady claimed to have prepared a very lengthy, thorough accounting of the whole past year, which she fully intended to read all the way through, but then disaster had struck! When she got out of her Chevy in the parking lot, the violent wind caught her right square in her report and it had probably blown clear to Visalia by that time. But she promised to try again, in time for the next meeting, and the membership seemed to know that they could count on it, unfortunately.

But back to my humble part in the program . . . Once I had somehow struggled through my prepared speech, and even gotten a few hearty laughs (not always in places where I thought laughs might be appropriate, for some peculiar reason), I decided to do what all other speakers always seem to do—ask for questions. Being polite, well-bred individuals, nobody asked me the obvious question, what was I doing trying to pass myself off as a speaker, although I'm sure many of them were seriously wonder-ing. But one lady immediately shot her arm up, waving it frantically, all the while performing explosive little half-leaps out of her seat (you know the type of maneuvers indicating that the instigator had spotted a blazing inferno or has to get to the rest room pronto). I thought it wise to recognize her, especially seeing as how hers was the only hand raised. She blurted out, "I think we're related!!!" Now that was one spunky little lady, to make that sort of damning admission right there in front of that whole audience. I'd always heard about these miraculous encounters. Heaven knows, we read about them every issue in *The Genealogical Helper* and elsewhere, so that we almost come to expect them, but this certainly was a first for me. She asked what counties in Kentucky my UNDERWOODs had hailed from. I told her Carter and Greenup. She shrieked with joy and asked, "Do you have any idea whatever happened to my great-aunt Beulah Mae after she ran off with that traveling salesman?" Having probably damaged my reputation enough for one day, all by myself, I quickly promised to meet her out in the hall after the meeting to sift through our family's ample dirty laundry.

Well, my next attempt at making a fool of myself came a few months later, with GAS (you must remember them by now?). Sacramento was only a cool 104 degrees that day but the audience was even warmer with its reception. That's the nice part about exposing yourself to folks who live in a town that's flooded with politicians. They get used to laughing a lot at almost anything. Or maybe their fruit punch was spiked again, I don't know, but they were a super audience and helped the butterflies to go away.

By the time Genealogical Publishing Company bought my book and took over the chore of promoting it, I'd been sent a few other invitations to speak, some of them even wanting me as the only speaker on the program, if you can swallow that. I know how it is, however. Sometimes program chairpersons get pretty desperate, don't you know, and make weird selections, especially if they've been at it too long and have run out of qualified speakers and/or money. As a consequence, I was well on the way toward becoming a little less petrified about the whole thing.

About that time I got a call from GPC saying that they had arranged to have three of their authors speak, as part of a panel presentation, at the prestigious American Library Association's Annual Conference in June in San Francisco. Amidst what appeared to me to be some pretty nervous laughter, they were asking me to be one of the speakers. WOW! That would be practically like being in Show Business! And that ought to give me two full months to get completely paralyzed with stage fright all over again.

Finally, the day I'd been so looking forward to, with great trepidation, dawned bright and clear. The arrangements agreed upon were that I would meet the publishing house representative, Joe GARONZIK, and the other two authors, at the Civic Auditorium, the spot where our ordeal was to take place. I figured it would be no problem for me to just drive my car up there from where I lived in San Jose. You can bet I was up bright and early that morning, eager as a turkey on the day before Thanksgiving, ready to give it my all, and praying that it would soon be over. As I sat at our kitchen table, trying to choke down breakfast between generous doses of thick, pink stomach-soother, I decided it might help take my mind off the impending catastrophe if I skimmed the morning newspaper. That's when I saw the announcement for the first time. Guess what they were going to be celebrating that day in San Francisco, besides the joyous coming together of frolicking librarians? *Gay/Lesbian Freedom Day!* In *San Francisco,* no less!!!

Not having ever been personally involved in one of

those, I didn't give the matter a second thought, not then I didn't anyhow. Tossing the newspaper on the sideboard, I heaved a massive sigh of doom and headed north. Comfortably familiar with San Francisco since my childhood days, I'd already made up my mind as to the best place to park my car for the morning—the Civic Center underground garage—if I was lucky and could find an empty space. Surprisingly, there were more spaces than there were parked cars when I descended into the garage, and I couldn't believe my luck. Then, as I made my lonely way up out of the garage and across the street, it seemed my guardian angel was still doing her job, because I hadn't been accosted by any muggers or rapists on the loose, and had only encountered two rather apathetic pan-handlers, who didn't seem to be putting very much effort into it and were easily discouraged. One thing I did notice, when crossing the street, was that there were sawhorses gaily (if you'll pardon the expression) scattered here and there, decorated with little printed signs saying "PARADE ROUTE." Since that information was no concern of mine, I simply ignored it and went on inside the Civic Auditorium.

As far as our panel presentation went, we were to be speaking to the genealogical librarians of America, those who chose to show up, that is, and anyone else who wandered into the room by mistake. When it came to the sequence of speakers, I had drawn a lousy straw and was scheduled fifth out of six speakers, giving me lots more time than I really required in which to fidget and get a dry mouth, and giving the members of the audience, if they chose to remain in the room that long, way more time than they probably needed to fall asleep before it was ever even my turn to cause them to do so. The first three speakers were librarians, wouldn't you know, and they discoursed freely (and well beyond their alloted time limits) about books, bookshelves, how to place them, where to place them, and so on. I guess you couldn't blame them. Passion sometimes seizes even a librarian, I suppose, and they can act like human beings too and get carried away.

The set-up for us authors was that Joe, who was probably the only one who had ever heard of us, would do the honors and introduce each of us. He proudly gave the impressive credits of the first author, John P. DERN, a distinguished and respected silver-haired gentleman who looked like what an author was supposed to look like. He had written a number of scholarly works, primarily about the great state of Maryland. And he was obviously an excellent speaker. I started asking myself, for the hundredth time, "What am I doing here?"

Then John sat down and Joe slowly got to his feet and gave me that look that told me plainly that he hoped I wouldn't screw up too much. As an introduction to my planned presentation, I decided to ad lib in something I had just made up. The reason for this last minute change was that the very boisterous parade had just started outside our windows and we couldn't help being aware of the festivities. So I said, "By the way, I'm afraid there is going to be more than a little confusion, due to that conflicting social event out there this morning, that massive parade. The 'Dykes on Bikes' offered me the loan of a Harley-Davidson if I would go over and join them. I guess it was my own fault . . . I mistook them for librarians." Well, you never saw anyone slink down in his chair so fast as that Joe GARONZIK did. Darn near must have been some kind of a record. And his face took on a shade of red that I couldn't even rightly identify, not being too much of a color expert. He may have been rehearsing his next introduction speech because he put his hand over his fore-head and started whispering to himself all the rest of the time I was up there. One sleeping member of the audience did wake up, however, and a person who had gone outside previously came back in, so hopefully I had some effect on someone other than poor Joe. At least my speech sort of seemed to get the librarians' attention, maybe because they wanted to see what other ding-dong thing I might spout off.

The final author/presenter of the morning was Bill DOLLARHIDE, a fine speaker with a great sense of humor and, luckily for all of us, the ability to pull the reputation of the publishing house back up out of the abyss I had undoubtedly sunk it into. Bill is the only one I know who can take a subject as deadly boring as the census boundaries and have you sitting on the edge of your chair listening to him talk about it. As a result, even Joe sat up straight again and recovered his ordinary hue.

Well, thank God, the agony was finally over and Joe announced we'd hop a jitney back to convention head-quarters across town in the Moscone Center. Trying to make amends, I offered to drive everyone back in my car. But when we got outside, it dawned on all of us that I might have a little problem. In fact, as it was explained to us by three of the biggest policemen I'd ever seen, who were standing in the middle of the intersection eyeing everything that moved with total hostility, I WOULDN'T BE MOVING MY CAR AT ALL THAT DAY, UNDERSTAND? Not until all those !@#$% ¢&*() were done with their (absolutely unprintable word) festivities, is the way they so delicately put it. Taking it all in, I began to have the sinking feeling that I might not see my car again for days.

Next we learned that the parade had only just begun. The exhaust fumes from the parade leaders, the "Dykes on Bikes," hadn't even settled, so we were in for a lot more colorful excitement. Because of the total gridlock, the jitneys were as grounded as everything else. So Joe suggested we walk to the first eating place we could find and have lunch, and the four of us did just that, locating a spot less than a block away. There was nothing too memorable about the lunch, except that Joe got stuck with the tab. The other two authors did start railing at him about the unusual delays they had encountered lately at the publishing house to get whatever it was that they needed. Joe, on the defensive, poked his thumb at me and proclaimed, "It's all *her* fault!" Almost choking on my linquine, I wondered what I'd done now, but Joe said it was just because my book was causing such a commotion back there that they were pretty bogged down. (I think that may have even been some kind of a left-handed compliment, but I'm not too sure?)

Our bellies filled, we ventured back out onto the sidewalk. Boy, were there sights in store for us! The parade was still wending its gay way up the street, forcing most vehicles to remain parked. Once again, it was my fault, I guess, because I came up with the totally brainless suggestion that it would do us good and provide healthy exercise to walk back to the Moscone Center (where we were supposed to be in less than an hour). So off we went, down the sidewalk, in a rather tightly-knit little squad. I don't know, maybe the fellows were feeling threatened, or something, because John kept trying to duck into a subway station, Bill never let up saying his feet were killing him and Joe just made a funny kind of constant groaning noise. Men are such complainers. They should have just been thankful they weren't wearing, as so many of the other fellows nearby were, high heels, like I was also stuck with. *Then* we would have heard complaining.

As it turned out, we got stuck walking the entire twenty-block, or whatever it was, parade route in reverse, so we saw almost everything there was to see, unfortunately. Since the library association had scheduled its events in the two widely separate downtown locations, the really dedicated librarians had been religiously hotfooting it back and forth between them all morning. But once the parade struck, there was a sudden, mysterious vanishing-act by most of the librarians. Actually, the more hysterical among them could be spotted hailing taxicabs headed for the airport, undoubtedly praying for an immediate flight back to Des Moines. The few who were still stubbornly hanging in there, hoofing it between Moscone and the Civic Center, stood out like lemonade salesmen at a heavy metal rock concert. First of all, in comparison with everybody else, they were dressed funny. Like undertakers. In contrast, the parade participants were exquisitely dolled up in sequins, feathers, balloons, satin, aluminum-foil, and ballerina tutus, and those were just the men. Some of the others had chosen complete combat fatigues, or, if they were feeling frivolous, two or three little poofs of material strategically placed hither and yon (with not nearly enough covering the yon). And they were all light-heartedly prancing down the street, some of them pretending to do the backstroke in unison, others perched precariously on floats full of flowers and bright crepe-paper streamers, most of them displaying a giddy *joie de vivre*.

The majority of the onlookers were not to be outdone either. Most of the celebrants crowding the sidewalks on our side of the street were sporting brief ensembles consisting primarily of leather and chains, with accessories resembling what your grandfather used to use to convince old Nellie to get the lead out. I'm not sure if these folks were truly enjoying the moving spectacle because very few of them were smiling, and many had looks on their faces like you would expect to see on Genghis KHAN on one of his bad days. But I suppose they were showing support, in their fashion. There were other little knots of people (mostly trying to stay out of the way of those with whips) accompanied by various animals, the majority of which were out of control in more ways than one, and I won't even begin to guess what they were there to represent. All in all, it was a very eye-opening, educational experience.

We survived the obstacle course and dragged our blistered feet into the Moscone Center, not a minute too soon. The main auditorium was completely filled with vendors' booths. The Genealogical Publishing Company booth was in the second-to-last row in the rear, about another mile-and-a-half away, or so it felt. We limped back there and relieved Roger SHERR, who had been manning the booth, so that he could go get a well-balanced meal from the hot dog stand.

I don't know how many of you have ever put in any duty in a booth at a convention or fair, but it was a brand-new experience for me. I'd never in my wildest imagination dreamed I'd ever have to confront that many roving librarians out on the town. With such an unbelievably large number of booths, covering such a huge area, only the very hardy or determined convention-goers ever made it all the way back to where ours was located. But when they did, they were in for a surprise. Joe knew that a booth way back in the hinterlands would have to come up with something outrageous to attract attention, or it would be dead in the water. So he'd had a monster-size poster-board done up, using a blowup of the cover of my book. And he had garish yellow tee-shirts, also representing the cover, tossed over everything that didn't move. That way, as the innocent librarian, usually with a weary, stupified, end-of-convention look on his or her face, rounded the partition dividing our corner booth from the next row, he or she was immediately hit with the gigantic bilious yellow communication: COLLECTING DEAD RELATIVES. I'll say this for it—it certainly drew them up short! So many of them decided to pose in front of it and have their picture snapped that Joe missed a bet not charging admission. But the nicest thing was that it generally got them to stop and chat and even buy some books.

I met the greatest bunch of librarians that afternoon. They were from all over the country. There was even one from Texas A&M University, my son's alma mater, so that should certainly lay to rest that tired old joke that Aggies only look at comic books. One small group, who seemed to be enjoying themselves and the conference immensely, were a dozen ladies who were all deaf. Our big sign launched them into a burst of frantic activity and they immediately "asked" us about it—the tee-shirts and some of the books. Unfortunately, none of us had learned to sign. Even so, with our own very inferior version of pointing and gesturing, we came to appreciate their visit and their delightful sense of humor.

That day was one I'll never forget. And it hadn't ended yet. Most booths were due to close at 5:00, or shortly afterwards, and ours was no exception. With each of us having commitments that would take us in separate directions and only two of us having cars (although that meant counting mine, which was still imprisoned), we had to do some planning. Bill DOLLARHIDE had already wisely

made his arrangements, probably fearing another endur-
ance contest on foot. So he bid our weary little bunch
adieu. Joe, John and Roger gallantly volunteered to escort
me back to the vicinity of where I had left my car. Our
taxi driver apologized that he couldn't drive much closer
than three blocks away from the Civic Center because the
streets any nearer were closed. "Uh-oh!", I thought, and
so did the other three. We pulled ourselves out of the taxi,
wondering what to do next.

The men suggested they would simply confide my predicament to some nearby officer and the officer would
surely agree to let me extricate my car from under the
Civic Center. But by the time we got to that swinging part
of town, it was more than obvious that my automobile
wouldn't be going anywhere at all, maybe not for a week.

We looked around us in amazement. There were color-
fully decorated booths, offering everything you could
imagine (and a lot more things you probably never in a
million years would ever imagine, no siree!), placed all

the way up and down the block in the middle of the street, definitely and completely blocking the exit from the parking garage. Then there was a gay (in every sense of the word) dance going on in the street in front of City Hall. Only men were dancing, of course, in the area closest to us, and the outskirts were being patrolled by what looked like the hit-squad contingent of glowering Dykes on Bikes.

The patrolling was effective because most of them looked like even Rambo wouldn't challenge them. On the outskirts of those outskirts sat the snarling cops on their motorcycles, looking more steamed up and on-the-prod than I could ever, in my wildest imagination, visualize your friendly neighborhood officers of the law ever looking. Well, you can bet that we aliens moved along like a glued-together unit, especially Roger, who hadn't been outside all day and didn't know what sights he was in for. Consequently, he stepped along danged sprightly, with his mouth hanging open like a yokel. They don't prepare you for that sort of thing back in Baltimore. About that time Roger spotted a makeshift canvas tent plopped down on the City Hall front lawn, with a hand-writ sign saying "FIRST-AID," and except for the fact that he probably feared being hauled bodily into the tent, he nearly had a case of vapors then and there. Joe just blurted out to me, "Don't you ever tell my wife I was out in all this or she won't come near me for the rest of the year."

Well, gentle reader, we did manage to get out of all the whoop-de-doo by finally locating John's car, illegally parked down an alley, thank goodness. John kindly chauffeured everyone to where he was going, through the nearly gridlocked traffic, and even delivered me safely clear down to my home in San Jose. My husband looked a little startled and asked, as husbands are prone to do, "What happened to the car this time?" After I laughingly described the situation and explained about the little trip we would have to make about midnight that night, he went into the bathroom and helped himself to some aspirins.

Anyway, you can accuse me of wandering just about as far as a person can wander off the subject of genealogy, and you'd certainly be right. But I will remind you that genealogy and libraries go together and we are doggoned lucky to have the libraries inhabited by librarians, and they go through plenty in order to go on doing what they do, you'll have to agree with that. And, to be frank, sometimes we genealogy hobbyists fall far short in the practice of formally acknowledging the librarians in our lives. So here's a "HIP! HIP! HOORAY!" for librarians, even if they do dress funny.

It's a bit of a contrast, if I do say so myself, to go from a riotous place like San Francisco in full bloom to what is obviously a much more sedate (maybe even stodgy) location, Ohio. Now before you "Buckeyes" start forming picket lines in front of my house, or lie down in front of any trains back there, or something, let me tell you that I'm as vocal as the rest of them when it comes to giving it to Ohio (did that come out right?).

"Experience is not what happens to you; it is what you do with what happens to you." — Aldous HUXLEY

Cruising the Ohio 200 Years Later

Only those of you who have personally stood on the sites of your ancestors' old stomping grounds will truly be able to identify with the spine-tingling thrill I felt when I received an invitation to go to Cincinnati, Ohio. Not all of you might feel so giddy about that particular spot, but my early Frenchman (or Italian, or whatever the heck he was) had landed at that very same historic metropolis (although it wasn't much of a metropolis then) almost exactly 200 years ago. Yes sir, whatever he may have been running from, he beached his trusty flatboat right there in the Cincinnati muck and never went back to wherever it was he'd started out from—presumably up-river.

The invitation that had worked me into such a frenzy asked me to go to Cincinnati in July to be a speaker at a national genealogical conference. (Little did I know then that only a madwoman would be caught dead in Cincinnati in July, due to their lovely weather, but I had a lot to learn.) As had been the case at the librarians' conference,

Genealogical Publishing Company was to be represented, and poor old Joe was to be once again blessed with trying to control me. Actually, I've got to tell you, he's a fairly non-threatening sort of fellow and spends most of his spare time trying to figure out ways to get such folks as the English and the Irish to stop lobbing incendiary devices at each other, and sit down and hug and kiss instead. He has the same visionary hopes for all other groups who hate each other's guts. In other words, Joe doesn't believe anyone should get hot under the collar about anything. So they just naturally stick him with all the unpleasant jobs.

When the long-awaited day arrived and I disembarked from the airplane in Kentucky (Kentucky? Yes, you see, Cincinnati refuses to recognize anything but boats), I wondered who had turned the blast furnace on. It was like a San Francisco bathhouse back there (well, maybe not *exactly* like one of those, but it was hot). By the time I got to the hotel across the river, I felt like I'd swum the entire distance. But enough complaints . . . I was ready for *FUN!* The first thing the planning committee did was to pack us speakers into station wagons, like sardines, and haul us out to some kind of wildly exhilarating museum, or library, or very solemn formal place, whatever it was. Cultured ladies in ruffly aprons were serving tea and crumpets and everyone was talking in whispers, like someone had died, and acting frightfully genteel. I accidentally laughed out loud at a remark I took to be humorous and Angus BAXTER looked at me like I'd broken wind, or something worse. After that, I tried doubly hard to emulate the rest of the crowd, not spill my tea on my imitation leopard-skin sweat shirt, and certainly not knowingly commit any other faux pox (or however that saying in Spanish goes?).

Now I don't know, fellow genealogists, if you can resist the Lorelei-call of that great temptation, the genealogical display booth, but I know for a fact that I sure can't. I even try to hide my money in my underwear, where I can't get to it without some pretty obscene movements, but it's no use. I'm a sucker for genealogy books. I don't even take the wise precaution of browsing through a book to see if, perchance, my surnames are in it (they never are, of course, so hunting in the index wouldn't help in the slightest). Besides, that sort of move would waste too much time that could be better spent just buying books willy-nilly, as fast as I can before some other eager customer can snatch them up first. In Cincinnati there was a whole floor of the goodies, and I had brought an empty steamer trunk, just in case. As you can guess, that's where I expensively toodled away the remainder of the afternoon.

Right after dinner that evening, we were once again put at the mercy of the planning committee, although in this instance they were offering one event I'd been dreaming about ever since I left California. The conference bigwigs had announced that they were going to send all the speakers down the Ohio River in a boat. This wasn't an attempt to rub us out, mind you, but some kind of a reward, I think. Sakes alive, if this wasn't the exact sort of experience to give me king-sized goose bumps, I don't know what was. Considering my great-great-great-grandfather had sailed these very same waters (well, maybe not the identical ripples of H_2O, but near enough) before 1790, you can bet I was about as fired up as a descendant could be. I pictured maybe even having some kind of psychedelic, out-of-body experience, the kind you sometimes read about, where I'd be catapulted back in time and be able to view the whole scene as it had been long ago. So I could hardly wait.

We almost missed the boat altogether, because we'd somehow gotten our ride assignments all mixed up. Accordingly, when Joe, Jan and I arrived at the docking spot, the riverboat had already pulled up its gangplank and was chugging away, and I had visions of having to swim for it. But the captain, probably on the lookout for strays, reversed direction and re-lowered the gangplank, thank goodness. Then, before we knew it, we were afloat.

In between trying to keep that handsome computer freak (discussed in an earlier chapter) hanging on my every word, and staying upright, I began to try to commune with the great beyond, in the hopes of summoning up the long-departed spirits of my ancestors. The first sign that something mystical might be starting to happen assailed my ears—a *very* loud manifestation of a ghostly pioneer cannon, being fired against the specters of the rampaging Indians, I swear it had to be. But before I could surrender in hallucinatory ecstasy, the computer hulk pricked my balloon with a more down-to-earth explanation. It seems that every time the dad-blasted Cincinnati

baseball team makes a touchdown, or whatever it is that baseball teams go gaga about, they fire a cannon. And, as luck would have it, that night was no exception, because apparently they were even then cavorting around performing their athletic shenanigans in Riverfront Stadium, near the spot from where we had shoved off. And they must have been playing their grandmothers that night because that cannon hardly ever let up. I prayed the cannonballs wouldn't sink the boat.

The romantic atmosphere of the full-mooned night on the river was also squelched by the incessant, cacophonous racket (which I refuse to dignify by calling music) blaring forth at top decibel out of the loudspeakers all over the boat. Whatever happened to quiet??? I don't think today's generation can even go to the bathroom unaccompanied by a deafening noise-inducement. My ancestors could probably hear the reverberations clear back 200 years ago, and I suspect that was why they were afraid to appear. I'll say one thing, it sure killed the ambiance for me. Put that together with screaming waterskiers whizzing back and forth alongside the boat and you couldn't conjure up an apparition if your life depended on it. So I had to settle for a conversation about computers and the visual display of parts of Kentucky and Ohio smoothly floating by. The only other pastime I could think of was to gaze down at the water and try to make a studious guess as to whether we were going up-river or down, unless it was crossways, and it probably didn't really matter at that point. But at my age one takes what thrills one can get.

The next morning was upon me much too soon and I very shakily made my way to my speaking assignment. Right after I was introduced someone pulled the plug on the microphone (probably on purpose), and there was a slight delay while the introducer and I got down on our hands and knees and groveled around for the cord in order to get re-connected. Now that sort of maneuver doesn't exactly insure the sense of dignity I like to establish right at the start of my speech, so maybe I should have just stayed down there, I don't know. Anyhow, by some miracle, I got through it without any other mechanical difficulties, and the audience was awfully kind and even tittered on occasion, behind their hands, so it was not too much of a nightmare.

Late that afternoon Genealogical Publishing Company had decided to go hog wild and throw a big wingding, sort of as a Grande Finale of the conference. It was called a "Meet the Authors" party, and GPC planned to bribe the conference attendees with food to force them to come. They arranged the *hors d'oeuvres* almost directly behind our table so that a person had to practically fall over an author to get to a canapé. I guess it worked because it was so crowded in there that we were picking anchovies out of our coiffures the rest of the evening. In my case, there were not only copies of my book to sign (if the need arose), but GPC had brought along more of those garish yellow tee-shirts as well. It was a puzzle to me whether I was expected to sign across the chests of anyone who might buy one of them, or what, but luckily, no one asked me to. For some strange reason, though, the tee-shirts went over especially well with the British in attendance, proving, as I always say, that there's no telling what will goose up an Englishman. Maybe they just wanted to take something back home to prove how uncivilized we still were here in the Colonies.

Well, at long last, the conference became history, but my Ohio adventures had only just begun. A dear friend,

Carolyn BLANKENSHIP, a hopelessly committed researcher and member of the D.A.R. (yes, there are a few of those still on speaking terms with me), had invited me to spend a couple of days at her home up in Miami County. She and her sister, Beatrice (also a D.A.R. member), had driven down to the conference that morning, not only to go on a wild spending spree in the exhibitors' area, but also to haul me back up north afterwards. We were minutes away from gathering up the last of my belongings from my hotel room and departing, when up pops a relative of mine, Glen GALEENER. He had driven straight through all the way from nearly Missouri to pay a visit and almost missed me altogether. Like I've said before, you just never can tell about relatives. They spring up like crabgrass, when you least expect it, even in a place as isolated as Ohio (they operate on some kind of a built-in radar, I do believe). In this case, all we could do was to ask him to play catch-up and follow us north for another two hours, if he wanted to chat. And, having inherited a good strong dose of the GALEENER bull-headedness, he did.

Leaving Glen as an unexpected, though welcome, guest at Beatrice's house in Greenville, Carolyn and I headed east towards her place. She had warned me previously that her home was filled to bursting with antiques and other things from times past that she couldn't quite bear to part with, so I was almost prepared—but not quite. Actually, I would have been happy as a clam to stay up all night and look at what could have passed for the inventory of a well-stocked antique shoppe, but Carolyn had suffered through a flood the night before in her living room and kitchen (Ohio weather being what it is) and wisely suggested we let the waters recede a bit till morning. She showed me to a guest room and we called it a night. It was a lovely, spacious bedroom, but I had a difficult time dropping off to sleep. I'm convinced the reason lay not so much in finding myself in an unfamiliar bed as in the slightly paranoid feeling that I was being watched. You see, the furnishings in the room were arranged in such a manner as to bring focus to bear on one main object, a huge oil portrait of Carolyn's late lawyer husband, glowering judiciously, as attorneys are prone to do, directly into the eyes of anyone

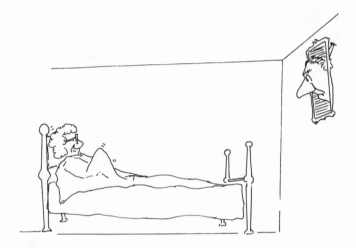

daring to trespass into that particular room. I mean, I felt like I was in the witness chair. Even with the lights off, he still seemed lit up and in charge. (Carolyn, if you ever read this, I'm only kidding, but next time perhaps you could drape a bandana over him, or something.) Finally, with a pillow over my head, I fell asleep.

The next day turned out to be chock-full of wild escapades. First of all, after a scrumptious breakfast prepared by Carolyn (the only cook I know who can remain cool up to her ankles in flood water), we left for a rendezvous in Indiana. We were scheduled to meet Beatrice, Glen and a distant cousin of mine, Sandra MUMAH, for lunch at a famous Richmond, Indiana landmark. Sandra, displaying the old GALEENER deviousness, had invited a very special local lady to be our guest. This invitee had the keys to one of the courthouses nearby (do you get the picture now?), so we got her just fortified enough with the bubbly to agree to let us into where they keep the records (there's more than one way to skin a key-keeper, ha ha).

None of us wanted to tear ourselves away from our personal rape of the courthouse records, but it was getting on in time and, besides, our hostess was fast sobering up. We were due back at the Garst Museum in Greenville, Ohio for a very special occasion. Since Greenville doesn't have a steady stream of celebrities passing through, not even those, like me, who could barely be identified with the word, someone had arranged for the local newspaper to meet us at the museum to do an interview. I chose to ride back to Ohio with Sandra and that was the first mistake. Sandra hadn't brought an umbrella and that was the second. I've never seen so much rain come down in my life before, all in the space of about a half-hour, and it got even worse by the time we arrived at the museum. The closest parking spot was half a block away, so you can probably imagine our condition when we stepped through the museum door. It may have come as something of a surprise to the innocent young Girl Scouts and Boy Scouts, formally attired in their pressed, *dry* uniforms, and standing at attention as the official welcoming envoys, to hear such colorful language issuing from the lips of two old broads, two absolutely *drenched* old broads. We were so wet, we left a river all the way to the rest room. Toni SEILER, the curator, and a startled young man in her office looked at us open-mouthed as we sloshed past, our thin summer clothes nearly transparent from the soaking. The man turned out to be the reporter, and let me tell you, that isn't the best way to make a good impression on the press (unless you are built like Marilyn MONROE). I will say this for him, and it was probably because of Ohio's obscenity laws, he did wait till I dried off somewhat before

he tried to take a picture. (Thanks to Toni's hospitality, we did spend a delightful afternoon discovering the treasures in that excellent museum, while drying out.)

After dinner there was to be an impromptu open-house, honoring me, to be held at Beatrice's house. Unfortunately, there was a mechanical combine and thresher show being held in the mud of the local municipal park, and it's not an easy thing competing with tractors and stuff like that in western Ohio. Folks from that neck of the woods know what's exciting and it doesn't always equate with dead relatives. But a number of loyal friends, who owed Beatrice one, I guess, did manage to get their cars unstuck and come out in the downpour to meet an author of dubious distinction and wolf down Beatrice's refreshments. I was certainly beholden to her for giving it the old college try.

Carolyn, not to be outdone by her sister, had promised me a sight I'd never forget later that night, but was keeping it a closely guarded secret. Since I was aware of her steadfast devotion to the D.A.R., and also to pioneer history and tradition, I guessed the locals might have torn themselves away from the threshers long enough to be staging a nighttime tableau of the Battle of Fallen Timbers, at the very least.

So, after we had bid a fond farewell to Beatrice and the last of her friends, this other little old lady and I hopped in her huge old 1960s automobile and headed straight for downtown Greenville, which is one main street about three blocks long. Finally, with a firm grip on the steering wheel, Carolyn uttered just one word, "Look!" And there in all its glory, in freshly washed and polished Chevys and Fords, was the cream of teenage Ohio engaged in the shocking practice of cruising! Well, Carolyn and I called it a night after about three spins down Main Street, ogling the teenagers who were staring back with even more bewilderment, wondering what in the world two such ancient hags were doing invading their turf, so to speak. My dear Ohio friend was firmly convinced that she had shown me the eighth wonder of the universe, a brand-new phenomenon I had never dreamed of. But when you come from California, I don't suppose there's much of anything considered shocking anymore. Now, maybe if she'd taken me to the combine and thresher bash, it would have been a different story.

So, after a long and fun-filled day, we headed our "cruiser" back to Carolyn's house, and with my appetite for excitement fully satiated, I thanked my hostess and retired to the Room of the Inquisitor. I quickly fell asleep. But not for long. I was rudely awakened by what sounded like a freight-train ramming the house, or maybe an airplane exploding on the roof. Frankly, whatever it was, I didn't think the house was long for this world. But danged if it wasn't just peculiar Ohio weather again, this time putting on a pyrotechnic display *extraordinaire*. I swear, I didn't think I'd live to see the morning, and I do believe even the lawyer closed his eyes and put his hands over his ears, the lightning was so bad. My guardian angel must have been tending to business because somehow I wasn't transformed into a frizzed ember and was able to survive and show up in one piece for breakfast.

Carolyn had saved a spectacular treat for after breakfast and had invited Glen and Sandra over so that they could also share. The flood had subsided in the living room far enough to enable Carolyn to wade in and rescue some of her very special old books (which she says she always keeps above high tide). The stars of the show, by far, had been in Carolyn's family since they'd first been created during the Civil War. They were the original hand-written medical journals of Dr. John Alexander JOBES of Greenville, and they gave all his patients' names and ailments and whether or not each had paid his bill. They also contained daily entries dating from the time the good doctor was called away to war, with his sad comments about the conditions he found there. These are absolutely priceless volumes and I certainly hope that someday they can be published so that they can be shared with historians and genealogy buffs nationwide. You can probably imagine the lumps Glen, Sandra and I had in our throats when we came across the entries for our own family members right there in the doctor's clear handwriting (wouldn't you know, our main ancestor hadn't paid his bill). That morning was by far the most precious reward of the whole trip to Ohio, thanks to Carolyn.

And an interesting postscript to the morning occurred later that day. Glen had graciously offered to drive me back to Cincinnati that afternoon, and we had said our reluctant goodbyes and left. Sandra, who had never met Carolyn before that weekend, was so engrossed in all the genealogical goodies that she remained behind, visiting with the two sisters and gorging herself on all the "new" records and information. All of a sudden, as they told me later, she let out a squeal of joy, recognizing a name she'd been searching for a long while, and the two JOBES descendants reacted with delighted surprise. What Sandra had just uncovered proved her not just a distant relative by marriage of the two sisters sitting there, but a blood relation! As those maddingly monotonous puppets down at Disneyland sing-songedly proclaim, "It's a small world after all!" That's the great thing about genealogy. Wonders never cease.

Well, with a sigh of relief, we will get ourselves out of Ohio and, with the shaky assistance of the United States Postal Service, take a big sedative and get ready to open our mail.

"You cannot write in the chimney with charcoal." —
Russian Proverb

Mail Monomania

According to my dictionary, the definition of monomania is "a mental disorder characterized by irrational
preoccupation with one subject." Gosh! Here I chose that
word because I thought that it pretty well described the
hangup of us genealogists with the product woefully dis-
tributed by the U.S. Postal authorities. But it sounds as if
it could just as accurately refer to our entire hobby. Oh
well, whoever wrote the dictionary probably didn't have
any ancestors at all, and so thought it was perfectly alright
to discriminate against those of us who do, especially
those of us who like to take an interest in them. That must
have been it. Well, we'll just go on our merry way and
zero in on whatever we please, and in this case, it's mail.

If there is one thing a genealogy hobbyist learns, right
from the day he or she timidly embarks as a lowly beginner, it is that without mail we may as well close up shop.
Probably the very first physical move each of us makes in
this hobby is toward a post office box to mail a letter. Boy,

I sure remember with embarrassment the first one I sent, word for word, in fact, because it was so bloody naive:

"Please send me a copy of the death certificate of my grandfather, Joseph Parent GALEENER. I think he died before 1930. Thank you."

That was it. No check enclosed. No nothing else. I could hardly supply an exact date, could I, when I didn't even know it and there was no one to ask. I did remember being told that he had died before I was born, and I knew he had lived his last years in the particular county to which I'd sent the simple request. Some departed soul up in heaven (maybe even old JPG himself?) must have been supervising the action and even assisting a little to get me started because, if you can believe in miracles, a copy of the death certificate was actually sent, accompanied by a small bill. Unheard of! Having my head screwed on a bit better today, as far as genealogy goes, I would never even attempt such a stupid move (but then I probably wouldn't get the certificate either, come to think of it). And it wasn't just that I was dealing with a county diametrically opposed to the policies under which all the other county offices in the United States operate either. I certainly found that out for a fact with the very next request I sent them. It was for a copy of the death certificate of Joseph's wife, my grandmother. In this case, I managed to have her name spelled in full and correctly, her maiden name included, her exact and correct date of death, and the exact and correct fee in the form of a check accompanying the whole mess. Three times I sent that same request to them and three times it was stubbornly returned with a curt note saying there was no such record in their jurisdiction. I later went in person to that particular county, which was only two hours away, thank goodness, and minutes after I walked through the portals of the county clerk's office I located the certificate right where it should be. So it's anyone's guess what happens to your mailed requests.

Granted, it's a lot tougher to get responses from mail sent to county courthouses nowadays than it was when I first turned myself loose in the hobby. County clerks, many of whom don't really look upon their exalted title as being synonymous with actual work, must be conniving together in some fashion in a mass vendetta aimed at putting every roadblock imaginable into the path of genealogists. So, as far as dealing with those personifications of frustration, you'll just have to come up with the best solutions yourself.

The letters we'll try to stumble around on mostly in this chapter are the ones we pen to one another. It might be best to divide these missives into those we direct to someone "new" in order to goose that individual into some action (such as sending along their bloody records, for goodness sake) and those we write to fellow hobbyists we've grown comfortable with and who may need bolstering from time to time to keep them hanging in there doing their share of the research.

Blimey if I'll ever, as long as I remain semi-rational and in this hobby, be able to come up with a fool-proof letter to send to those totally lethargic, uncooperative folks who simply will not answer your letters no matter how many you send to them! I'm waiting for one right now, and have been for six months. As always seems to be the case, unfortunately, she is the very first contact I've had with anyone at all from a certain great-aunt's branch, and she lives too far away for me to go threaten her in person. The funny thing is that she initially contacted me, not the reverse, and appeared to be frightfully enthusiastic. She alluded briefly, in the text of her letter, to what sounded like an absolutely fascinating, though tragic, family encounter with the infamous Bonnie and Clyde, and then ended the short reference with, "But I'm sure you have

already heard that story." Well, since I'd never even been in touch with any other descendant from that line, I had also never heard the story (and now I wonder if I ever will). In my immediate letter back to her I begged her to share it, and any other information and records she cared to send about her branch. I'm still waiting. I hope she hasn't gone and died, not just now, at such a crucial time, at least not before she's had the chance to cough up her information. The only other answer I can think of, that might explain her silence, is that she had initially gotten in touch by sending a check and a request to purchase a copy of the family history. Since her brief mention of the Bonnie and Clyde shooting would indicate that the particular relative/victim involved may have been one of the very few members of our colorful family who were identified as being on the side of the law in any shootout, maybe she has taken offense at finding the family history peppered with those who weren't. I don't know, perhaps she was expecting me to prove a family connection to Queen Elizabeth, or someone, but since Queen Elizabeth isn't generally known for stealing horses, that may be impossible.

There have been others over the years who just simply have *never* written back. The aggravating part of this problem is that they always represent a branch of your family for which you have no other living contact. It seems to be a rule. If you only knew a sister or a brother of theirs, a neighbor, or even their hairdresser, you could at least find out if they had been hauled away someplace, for whatever reason, and were not just being stubborn. In the case of my latest non-correspondent, she even admitted that she wasn't "the letter-writer in the family" (and boy, do I believe it now). She did say her sister was prolific in this regard, but then she coyly neglected to give me either her sister's name or the necessary address. I think she is trying to drive me crazy, is what I think.

On rare occasions, in other instances of this same type of frustration, I've been successful by just hanging in there and pestering the procrastinator until they succumb to my demands (before they succumb altogether), usually because it finally strikes them as being less troublesome than to go on enduring the continual hounding. So, fellow hobbyist, harassment sometimes pays off.

One of the nicest side-effects of our hobby is that you will rarely have an empty mailbox again. The only trouble is, if you're as slow about it as I am, you may never see the last of that pile of letters which need answering. But don't get me wrong, for once this isn't meant to be a whining complaint. At first I didn't know if I'd ever be able to keep up with my fellow researchers/letter writers, but I soon learned to look with eager anticipation for their incoming dispatches, not only because we'd become good buddies but also because you never know what exciting goodies the envelopes might contain from month to month and then from year to year on the family research. So you wind up interrupting whatever you might be doing the instant the mailman makes his daily deposit. At least I do.

I will admit that one subject, seemingly a favorite with genealogists for some strange reason, used to get my goat some years ago. I'm referring to the letter one receives containing perhaps fifteen hand-written pages, fourteen-and-a-half of which are filled with the writer's miseries. I've mellowed on that score lately, however, possibly because I can now match the worst of them page-for-page with ailments of my own. As a matter of fact, I'm presently typing this chapter with one finger of my left hand, and not because I think it's fun that way. I have had the rotator-cuff surgery I mentioned in an earlier chapter, and my right arm is taped down snug to my body and may never see action again, the way it feels. Quite frankly, I'm taking so many pills these days that I wouldn't be a bit surprised to have the local sheriff's deputies and their specially-trained dogs burst through my door and ask if they might get in some practice performing a drug raid (not that the lawmen in this part of California need any practice doing that sort of thing, it's sad to say). No, I've become pretty sympathetic in my old age when it comes to filling pages of stationery full of aches and pains, maybe because that seems to be the first thing that comes to mind each day. So please remember, whatever subject you choose to dwell upon, the important thing is to keep writing.

As an example of my own incoming mail, there is one close friend (and I hope she goes on being a close friend

after I've told this story) who never ceases to amaze me. When she started corresponding with me a few years ago, I thought the woman was sending me full-length manuscripts in the mail. I mean, I doubt that I could turn out twenty-five page letters, and some longer, if my life depended on it. But after a while, I became so addicted to the hefty espistles that on the rare occasions when she just jots down quickies of ten pages or so, I somehow feel cheated. The greatest thing about them is that they are filled with her always slightly cockeyed adventures, and believe me, she's a magnificent story teller. She makes me feel like I'm right there beside her, taking part in her zany life. Whatever happens in the future, I hope she keeps them coming.

Now, a word of warning. If you ever go so far as to write a book, and your address is somehow listed on the reverse of the title-page (as well it should be if your book is to be self-published and you ever expect to attract any orders), you'd best be prepared for all sorts of interesting mail, some of it extremely welcome and some of it pretty far out. This fact certainly helped me quite a lot after I gave birth to my 718-page family history, because it put me in touch not only with potential purchasers but also with brand new contacts within the family, both fellow researchers and just plain onlookers.

But when I really began receiving weird stuff in my mailbox was right after I self-published the first edition of *Collecting Dead Relatives*. Don't get me wrong, there weren't any threats, live rattlesnakes, or anything like that (leastways not yet, and I hope this doesn't give anyone any funny ideas). No, most of the mail has been from individuals who had little stories of their own connected with genealogy, often quite hilarious ones, that they felt like sharing. For instance, there was the lady who claimed she always attracted fleas in cemeteries (so does my dog, so I can certainly sympathize with her). And there was the gentleman who owned up to weighing in at twenty-two stone, who was not (understandably) very agile. His little escapade involved being locked up in a high-walled grave-yard all night long. His main concern seemed to be that he'd neglected to bring along any food.

Admittedly, there have been a handful of mailed com-munications which have been a shade more spacy than those above, causing me to check the return address on the envelope to determine whether it wasn't from a nurs-ing home, drug rehabilitation center, or some similar type of establishment. But even this kind of letter means that someone spent time, effort, and a 25¢-stamp on it, and that sort of activity is still a whole lot more productive than to sit there and stare at the walls.

One form of treasure brought by the mailman that always makes me want to sing (except, since I am, with-out a doubt, the world's most abysmal vocalist, I would never try it) is the genealogical society periodical. I sub-scribe to lots more of these than makes any kind of sense, I suppose, because I almost never find my surnames in any of them, but they are pure excitement, nevertheless. My very favorite one is the *Tree Shaker,* put out by the East-ern Kentucky Genealogical Society. Maybe that's because Evelyn Scyphers JACKSON, an excellent author in her own right, holds down the job of editor. She always seems to juggle things around each issue so as to have just the right balance of stories, records, queries, etc., to keep it interesting. I'll have to ask her someday just what side her eastern Kentucky ancestors were on during my family's feuding back there, but I've hesitated doing so to date for fear she might come up with the wrong answer and I'd have to burn the periodical to prove my family loyalty.

Well, dear reader, it's almost time to head this book back to the barn. I hope you'll excuse the buffoonery.

Even in genealogy it doesn't hurt to giggle now and then. Before you go for good, permit me to get down to serious business once again and dictionary up your vocabulary . . .

> *"A sense of humor keen enough to show a man his own absurdities, as well as those of other people, will keep him from the commission of all sins, or nearly all, save those that are worth committing."* — Samuel BUTLER

Words to Set You Apart (Probably Far Apart)

The following words were lifted (with the greatest of care) off assorted death certificates, plagiarized out of an 1875 medical book*, snatched out of the smoggy, blue sky, and maybe even invented (can't be choosy). If you stubbornly insist on continuing in this hobby, there might even come a day when you'll find yourself openly confronted with these very same words, and then where will you be? Accordingly, you should practice them in the library on people who try to act superior. Please don't ask me how to pronounce them. It took all my limited faculties just to spell most of the little devils.

Animalcular—This is what people are who keep claiming to see teeny, tiny animals floating around that no one else can see.

---

* *The People's Common Sense Medical Adviser*, by R. V. PIERCE, M.D. Now those sneering monsters who write book reviews can't say this studious tome lacks a ~~bibliography bibliopolist bibulosophy~~ (nuts!) book list.

159

Anthelmintic—If your ancestor was advised to swill down a flagon of this stuff, it meant he had worms, and I don't mean in his garden.

Bilious Colic—My dictionary says bilious means "bad tempered and cross," and your predecessor had every right to be if his blooming bile ducts were running amok. Colic means "seated in the colon," which I think is just south of the semi-colon and wanders down into territory that shouldn't be discussed freely in a family book.

Certified—What you have to do to documents to be admitted to the D.A.R. and what they used to do to individuals to be admitted to insane asylums. There's probably no connection. Some paid genealogists claim they are, and some of them certainly should be.

Combine—Monstrosities Nebraskans and Iowans choose to put out on their front lawns as decorations instead of those much classier, brightly-colored concrete pixies, deer and Virgin Marys so popular here in California. I think their prime use (the combines, not the Virgin Marys) is to do something unmentionable to the soy beans or millet or vetch or whatever all that stuff is covering Kansas, Iowa and places like that.

Consumption—If a healthy woman is turned loose in a department store (especially at the frenzied height of a sale), she is a sure bet to become guilty of the consumption of too many goods and services, and in some cases too much of this type of activity can make her waste away like Camille.

Creosote—The above-mentioned medical book declares, "This is a powerful antiseptic." (???) Boy, and I always thought all you did with it was to brush it on things you wanted to bury in the ground, like fenceposts, while you kept a good strong grip on your nose.

Dropsy—Does not refer to when clumsy oafs have accidents with the good china or crystal. If the doctor wrote down on the record that your ninety-pound Zachariah "swole up like a balloon," this is probably what ailed the poor fellow.

Female Weakness—Menfolks undoubtedly thought the little woman was just malingering. After all, all she'd done was to have fifteen kids in sixteen years (he'd had to go to war one year), cook, can, clean, sew, wash, iron, plant and harvest the south forty, tend the younguns, shoot Indians when they became too pesky, and milk ten cows daily, among other easy chores. But, lo and behold, one night when he came back from the local tavern he found her *sitting down doing nothing!!!* "Whatcha sittin there for, Martha, it's only 10 o'clock?" A good purge of ipecac and/or a strong charge from the static electrical machine usually set her to rights again.

Genetics—What you wish your ancestors had paid more attention to while they were at it so you wouldn't have so many problems to contend with today.

Historical Site—Conveniently located next to a parking lot, this was usually a place where a great number of pioneers got themselves slaughtered, sometimes for reasons almost forgotten now, which we drill into our young children the importance of remembering (and some of them actually do, right up until the day they take the test).

Hops—Used to be considered a red-hot way to put an insomniac to sleep. All you had to do was take a bag of the leaves, moisten with whiskey and put it under your head (it helped, I guess, to be lying down when you performed this maneuver or some nearby knave might snatch it away from you, run off behind the barn and smoke it).

This concoction was supposed to make you feel no pain. Maybe the fumes would do it? But I suspect the fellow claiming to be following this prescription just told his wife this is what the doctor advised him to do, when she caught him at it. Nobody in his right mind would waste good whiskey this way. You could probably achieve the same effect if you ate the leaves and washed them down with the whiskey.

Hung—Contrary to what some of you think this expression refers to in modern times, when found on an old death certificate, it actually meant "well-endowed with a section of hemp in the vicinity of one's neck."

Immigrant—I get this all mixed up with emigrant and eminent, which I think means high, and impotent, which certainly doesn't mean high by a long shot. I do believe that one of these words was the polite term used for alien in the olden days, when we needed lots of them to fill in the space, but now that the space is filled to overflowing it would help a great deal if some of the immigrants would just transform themselves into emigrants and go away before the whole place sinks into the ocean.

Index Cards—Little 3x5 things you wish your relatives would stay on and not come for visits. When you've gotten about 1,000 of them all painstakingly alphabetized, clutched in your hand and ready to put in your card file, it is an absolute guarantee that you will stumble with them or get caught in a high wind.

Informant—In police parlance this person could be called a squealer, a snitch, or quite often a name that is totally unprintable. So, too, an individual so designated on a death certificate can be referred to in equally vulgar language if he or she was especially thick-headed and indulged in the persistent and vexatious use of the term "unknown" for each blank he or she was asked to fill in.

Ischemia—Something that happened to poor peasants who lived in Transylvania and lacked the good sense to stay away from vampires.

Logwood—This is what early-day physicians prescribed "to remedy the relaxed condition of the bowels," if you get the meaning, because it produced "the sensation known as puckering." The book didn't elucidate whether you were supposed to whittle it, shove it somewhere, or attack it with a chain saw, but if you were successful, I presume you were rewarded with puckered bowels.

Mustered—This is not something you smear on hot dogs. It is a term found on almost all old military records. Since the start of history the military bigwigs have racked their brains trying to come up with fancy words that civilians wouldn't be able to understand, and this is just another pitiful example. It means herding a bunch of reluctant, if not downright ready-to-bolt, hayseeds together and telling them, "You're in the army now!"

Myocarditis—If your ancestor had the misfortune to possess a myocardium which got stuck in the doorjamb, you could almost count on it resulting in an empty seat at the old dinner table. Anything with "card" in it had better be treated with respect because it rarely refers to a poker game.

Pension—My dictionary says the definition of this word is "to hang." We can accept that. If the poor shot-up soldier, or his widow, could hang in there long enough to outlast those infernal Washington bureaucrats (still no easy task to this day), a wildly generous windfall of maybe even as much as $82.50 per year would be granted to the veteran so that he could then proceed to live high on the hog.

Piles—What you have a lot of before you put it in your briefcase. I haven't been able to locate my dining room table for years now due to this problem. Don't let your notes and records stack up on you or they are apt to get out of control and you may never find anything again.

Reg.—This is not generally intended as a nickname for chaps named Reggie. I was going to give you the expert opinion that it meant regiment, leastways on old military records, but doggoned, whoever wrote my dictionary has me completely befuddled because they claim it stands for regent, region, register, regular, regulation, regurgitate, syncopation . . . *syncopation*??? Anyway, just go ahead and take your pick.

Rev.—When you see this designation regarding military records circa 1775-1783, it probably doesn't mean to accelerate your engine. Although it could mean the good *Rev*erend ran away with the *rev*enue causing the *rev*iew board to go into a *rev*olving fit, it most likely refers to our spirited *rev*enge on those dastardly British (better known as a mad *rev*ulsion in England) and dubbed the *Rev*olution in the Colonies (which some old-school British still call us). Are you still following this scholarly discussion?

Senility—I think this refers to a superior mentality because I've found it used quite often in records concerning *my* branch of the family. My dictionary says it means "nearing the end of an erosion cycle," but I don't understand that at all since none of my family members so stricken spent much time out in the fields plowing incorrectly, or doing whatever it is that causes erosion, so whoever wrote the dictionary must not have been rowing with both oars by the time he got to the "S" section.

Shaking Palsy—A condition caused by too many home treatments with the good old static electrical machine.

Shot—If your relatives were fine, upstanding members of the community, like mine, this term may have been listed on occasion as the cause of their demise. I am guessing that it was not usually intended as the slang expression we know in modern times, meaning "worn out," but was probably the end result of a little spirited horseplay involving flying bullets.

St. Vitus's Dance (Chorea)—Unfortunately, the symptoms of this malady have been picked up by today's teenagers, who refer to it as "hard rock." Now if we could only find a modern purge.

Static Electrical Machine—(Say, this little gadget might just cure the ailment directly above.) But seriously, this thing is a mysterious little black box with a jumble of scientific little wires and electrodes, usually used as a threat to malingerers, and quite often with a great deal of success. After the initial "treatment," once you got your hair to lay back down flat again, you rarely confessed to being bothered by many diseases in the future, not out loud anyway.

Thresher—A person who thrashes around, by himself or with a friend, out in the cornfields. He tends to do it double-speed if he's caught off-guard by the sudden, unexpected approach of a combine on the loose. Sometimes this term was listed on old records as an occupation, although why anyone would voluntarily own up to this type of scandalous activity is beyond comprehension.

Tippling—If your ancestor was thrown in the slammer a lot, and this was inevitably listed as the cause, you can be reasonably certain that he wasn't currently heading the local temperance crusade and may have even been inbibing something a tad stronger than sassafras tea. Of course, he was undoubtedly doing it "for medicinal purposes only."

Tippling House—Where you went in the early days to get your prescriptions filled.

Typhoid Fever—What you hoped you'd get in the Civil War so the generals wouldn't send you to the front lines to serve as a magnet for a Minié ball. Lots of them got their wish.

Vaccinia—You can get this by messing around too much with your cow. (Are you listening, you genealogists up there in Wisconsin and Minnesota?) But they probably did this deliberately in the olden days because it sure beat the kind you got from humans *(Variola)*.

Vapors, The—What you can still get close to income tax time. This term was what delicate females said they had in the good old days just before they swooned dead away in the parlor. They probably used it to get something they wanted out of men.

Vol.—If that well-worn military record you are studying says your ancestor was in the Connecticut Vol. Inf., I can tell you right here and now that he was in big trouble because Vol. means volcano. And since Inf. means infinitive, it would be easier to just split and not try to come up with an explanation for this mess. But actually, in this case, Vol. stands for "Volunteers," which is what the War Department jokingly called all the poor young lads who were rounded up and forced into the army.

HAPPY HUNTING!